Mark Water

BIBLE STUDY

made simple

AMG
Publishers

God's Word is our highest calling.

AMG Publishers
6815 Shallowford Road
Chattanooga, Tennessee 37421

ISBN 0-89957-428-9

Designed by Andrew Milne Design

Printed in China.

Contents

Introduction

Augustine of Hippo wrote, "The depth of the Christian Scriptures is boundless. Even if I were attempting to study them and nothing else, from boyhood to decrepit old age, with the utmost leisure, the most unwearied zeal, and with talents greater than I possess, I would still be making progress in discovering their treasures."

This volume centers on the treasures of the Bible referred to by the fourth-century bishop of Hippo. The purpose of *Bible Study Made Simple* is to give you dozens of do-it-for-yourself Bible studies so that you can train yourself in the art of Bible study in a systematic and enriching way.

Today we have more resources for studying God's word than ever before. It just may be that our greatest problem is getting around to studying the Bible. Augustine had something to say about this as well: "Will is to grace as the horse is to the rider." Francis Bacon once said: "Too many develop every talent except the most vital one of all, the talent to use their talents: will-power." This book is guaranteed to build you up spiritually because its gives you 101 ways to get the best out of God's Word.

1 STUDYING AND READING THE BIBLE

CONTENTS	
	page

Introduction

Surprisingly few Christians have ever read the Bible from cover to cover. Where should we start? For those who would like to try this, Part 1 begins with a Bible reading plan devised and used by the godly Scottish minister, Robert Murray M'Cheyne (1813-43). Those who follow his Bible reading schedule will read through the Old Testament once and the New Testament and Psalms twice in a year.

R. A. Torrey was appointed by D. L. Moody to be the first head of what we today know as the Moody Bible Institute. Torrey's basic methods for studying the Bible are now given, together with some examples of ways of studying particular passages. You'll need a pencil and notebook here, if you want to derive maximum benefit from his methods of Bible study. This chapter then includes some straightforward Bible studies.

Some of the numerous helpful methods of Bible study are then explained. Examples of the "microscopic" approach to Bible study and the "telescopic" approach to Bible study are given. It is easy to misinterpret the Bible, so some of the basic principles which help us to interpret it correctly are therefore also given in this section.

Some people think that it is almost irreverent or perhaps distracting to write on the pages of a Bible, while others like to write notes all over their Bibles to remind them of important points they have heard or thought. For the latter group, a systematic set of Bible markings and symbols has been provided as an aid to Bible study.

It is not possible to follow through the Bible studies in this book without agreeing with the psalmist who said that he loved God's word "more than gold, more than pure gold" (Psalm 119:127).

Reading through the Bible in one year

JANUARY THRU' FEBRUARY					
JANUARY			**FEBRUARY**		
Date	*Morning*	*Evening*	*Date*	*Morning*	*Evening*
01	Genesis 1, Matthew 1	Ezra 1, Acts 1	01	Genesis 33, Mark 4	Esther 9, 10, Romans 4
02	Genesis 2, Matthew 2	Ezra 2, Acts 2	02	Genesis 34, Mark 5	Job 1, Romans 5
03	Genesis 3, Matthew 3	Ezra 3, Acts 3	03	Genesis 35, 36, Mark 6	Job 2, Romans 6
04	Genesis 4, Matthew 4	Ezra 4, Acts 4	04	Genesis 37, Mark 7	Job 3, Romans 7
05	Genesis 5, Matthew 5	Ezra 5, Acts 5	05	Genesis 38, Mark 8	Job 4, Romans 8
06	Genesis 6, Matthew 6	Ezra 6, Acts 6	06	Genesis 39, Mark 9	Job 5, Romans 9
07	Genesis 7, Matthew 7	Ezra 7, Acts 7	07	Genesis 40, Mark 10	Job 6, Romans 10
08	Genesis 8, Matthew 8	Ezra 8, Acts 8	08	Genesis 41, Mark 11	Job 7, Romans 11
09	Genesis 9, 10, Matthew 9	Ezra 9, Acts 9	09	Genesis 42, Mark 12	Job 8, Romans 12
10	Genesis 11, Matthew 10	Ezra 10, Acts 10	10	Genesis 43, Mark 13	Job 9, Romans 13
11	Genesis 12, Matthew 11	Nehemiah 1, Acts 11	11	Genesis 44, Mark 14	Job 10, Romans 14
12	Genesis 13, Matthew 12	Nehemiah 2, Acts 12	12	Genesis 45, Mark 15	Job 11, Romans 15
13	Genesis 14, Matthew 13	Nehemiah 3, Acts 13	13	Genesis 46, Mark 16	Job 12, Romans 16
14	Genesis 15, Matthew 14	Nehemiah 4, Acts 14	14	Genesis 47, Luke 1:1-38	Job 13, I Corinthians 1
15	Genesis 16, Matthew 15	Nehemiah 5, Acts 15	15	Genesis 48, Luke 1:39-80	Job 14, I Corinthians 2
16	Genesis 17, Matthew 16	Nehemiah 6, Acts 16	16	Genesis 49, Luke 2	Job 15, I Corinthians 3
17	Genesis 18, Matthew 17	Nehemiah 7, Acts 17	17	Genesis 50, Luke 3	Job 16, 17, I Corinthians 4
18	Genesis 19, Matthew 18	Nehemiah 8, Acts 18	18	Exodus 1, Luke 4	Job 18, I Corinthians 5
19	Genesis 20, Matthew 19	Nehemiah 9, Acts 19	19	Exodus 2, Luke 5	Job 19, I Corinthians 6
20	Genesis 21, Matthew 20	Nehemiah 10, Acts 20	20	Exodus 3, Luke 6	Job 20, I Corinthians 7
21	Genesis 22, Matthew 21	Nehemiah 11, Acts 21	21	Exodus 4, Luke 7	Job 21, I Corinthians 8
22	Genesis 23, Matthew 22	Nehemiah 12, Acts 22	22	Exodus 5, Luke 8	Job 22, I Corinthians 9
23	Genesis 24, Matthew 23	Nehemiah 13, Acts 23	23	Exodus 6, Luke 9	Job 23, I Corinthians 10
24	Genesis 25, Matthew 24	Esther 1, Acts 24	24	Exodus 7, Luke 10	Job 24, I Corinthians 11
25	Genesis 26, Matthew 25	Esther 2, Acts 25	25	Exodus 8, Luke 11	Job 25, 26, I Corinthians 12
26	Genesis 27, Matthew 26	Esther 3, Acts 26	26	Exodus 9, Luke 12	Job 27, I Corinthians 13
27	Genesis 28, Matthew 27	Esther 4, Acts 27	27	Exodus 10, Luke 13	Job 28, I Corinthians 14
28	Genesis 29, Matthew 28	Esther 5, Acts 28	28	Exosus 11, 12:21, Luke 14	Job 29, I Corinthians 15
29	Genesis 30, Mark 1	Esther 6, Romans 1			
30	Genesis 31, Mark 2	Esther 7, Romans 2			
31	Genesis 32, Mark 3	Esther 8, Romans 3			

Robert Murray McCheyne

Robert Murray McCheyne compiled this Bible reading schedule in 1842. There are four Bible readings for each day, two in the morning and two in the evening, which will take you through the Old Testament once and the New Testament and Psalms twice, in a year.

MARCH THRU' APRIL

MARCH			APRIL		
Date Morning		Evening	Date Morning		Evening
01	Exodus 12:22-51, Luke 15	Job 30, I Corinthians 16	01	Leviticus 4, Psalms 1, 2	Proverbs 19, Colossians 2
02	Exodus 13, Luke 16	Job 31, 2 Corinthians 1	02	Leviticus 5, Psalms 3, 4	Proverbs 20, Colossians 3
03	Exodus 14, Luke 17	Job 32, 2 Corinthians 2	03	Leviticus 6, Psalms 5, 6	Proverbs 21, Colossians 4
04	Exodus 15, Luke 18	Job 33, 2 Corinthians 3	04	Leviticus 7, Psalms 7, 8	Proverbs 22, I Thessalonians 1
05	Exodus 16, Luke 19	Job 34, 2 Corinthians 4	05	Leviticus 8, Psalm 9	Proverbs 23, I Thessalonians 2
06	Exodus 17, Luke 20	Job 35, 2 Corinthians 5	06	Leviticus 9, Psalm 10	Proverbs 24, I Thessalonians 3
07	Exodus 18, Luke 21	Job 36, 2 Corinthians 6	07	Lev. 10, Psalms 11, 12	Proverbs 25, I Thessalonians 4
08	Exodus 19, Luke 22	Job 37, 2 Corinthians 7	08	Lev. 11, 12, Psalms 13, 14	Proverbs 26, I Thessalonians 5
09	Exodus 20, Luke 23	Job 38, 2 Corinthians 8	09	Lev. 13, Psalms 15, 16	Proverbs 27, 2 Thessalonians 1
10	Exodus 21, Luke 24	Job 39, 2 Corinthians 9	10	Lev. 14, Psalm 17	Proverbs 28, 2 Thessalonians 2
11	Exodus 22, John 1	Job 40, 2 Corinthians 10	11	Lev. 15, Psalm 18	Proverbs 29, 2 Thessalonians 3
12	Exodus 23, John 2	Job 41, 2 Corinthians 11	12	Lev. 16, Psalm 19	Proverbs 30, 1 Timothy 1
13	Exodus 24, John 3	Job 42, 2 Corinthians 12	13	Lev. 17, Psalms 20, 21	Proverbs 31, 1 Timothy 2
14	Exodus 25, John 4	Proverbs 1, 2 Corinthians 13	14	Lev. 18, Psalm 22	Ecclesiastes 1, 1 Timothy 3
15	Exodus 26, John 5	Proverbs 2, Galatians 1	15	Lev. 19, Psalms 23, 24	Ecclesiastes 2, 1 Timothy 4
16	Exodus 27, John 6	Proverbs 3, Galatians 2	16	Lev. 20, Psalm 25	Ecclesiastes 3, 1 Timothy 5
17	Exodus 28, John 7	Proverbs 4, Galatians 3	17	Lev. 21, Psalms 26, 27	Ecclesiastes 4, 1 Timothy 6
18	Exodus 29, John 8	Proverbs 5, Galatians 4	18	Lev. 22, Psalms 28, 29	Ecclesiastes 5, 2 Timothy 1
19	Exodus 30, John 9	Proverbs 6, Galatians 5	19	Lev. 23, Psalm 30	Ecclesiastes 6, 2 Timothy 2
20	Exodus 31, John 10	Proverbs 7, Galatians 6	20	Lev. 24, Psalm 31	Ecclesiastes 7, 2 Timothy 3
21	Exodus 32, John 11	Proverbs 8, Ephesians 1	21	Lev. 25, Psalm 32	Ecclesiastes 8, 2 Timothy 4
22	Exodus 33, John 12	Proverbs 9, Ephesians 2	22	Lev. 26, Psalm 33	Ecclesiastes 9, Titus 1
23	Exodus 34, John 13	Proverbs 10, Ephesians 3	23	Lev. 27, Psalm 34	Ecclesiastes 10, Titus 2
24	Exodus 35, John 14	Proverbs 11, Ephesians 4	24	Numbers 1, Psalm 35	Ecclesiastes 11, Titus 3
25	Exodus 36, John 15	Proverbs 12, Ephesians 5	25	Numbers 2, Psalm 36	Ecclesiastes 12, Philemon
26	Exodus 37, John 16	Proverbs 13, Ephesians 6	26	Numbers 3, Psalm 37	Song of Sol. 1, Hebrews 1
27	Exodus 38, John 17	Proverbs 14, Philippians 1	27	Numbers 4, Psalm 38	Song of Sol. 2, Hebrews 2
28	Exodus 39, John 18	Proverbs 15, Philippians 2	28	Numbers 5, Psalm 39	Song of Sol. 3, Hebrews 3
29	Exodus 40, John 19	Proverbs 16, Philippians 3	29	Numbers 6, Psalms 40, 41	Song of Sol. 4, Hebrews 4
30	Leviticus 1, John 20	Proverbs 17, Philippians 4	30	Numbers 7, Psalms 42, 43	Song of Sol. 5, Hebrews 5
31	Leviticus 2, 3, John 21	Proverbs 18, Colossians 1			

MAY THRU' JUNE

MAY			JUNE		
Date	Morning	Evening	Date	Morning	Evening
01	Numbers 8, Psalm 44	Song of Sol. 6, Hebrews 6	01	Deuteronomy 5, Psalm 88	Isaiah 33, Revelation 3
02	Numbers 9, Psalm 45	Song of Sol. 7, Hebrews 7	02	Deuteronomy 6, Psalm 89	Isaiah 34, Revelation 4
03	Numbers 10, Psalms 46, 47	Song of Sol. 8, Hebrews 8	03	Deuteronomy 7, Psalm 90	Isaiah 35, Revelation 5
04	Numbers 11, Psalm 48	Isaiah 1, Hebrews 9	04	Deuteronomy 8, Psalm 91	Isaiah 36, Revelation 6
05	Numbers 12, 13, Psalm 49	Isaiah 2, Hebrews 10	05	Deuteronomy 9, Psalms 92, 93	Isaiah 37, Revelation 7
06	Numbers 14, Psalm 50	Isaiah 3, 4, Hebrews 11	06	Deuteronomy 10, Psalm 94	Isaiah 38, Revelation 8
07	Numbers 15, Psalm 51	Isaiah 5, Hebrews 12	07	Deuteronomy 11, Psalms 95, 96	Isaiah 39, Revelation 9
08	Numbers 16, Psalms 52-54	Isaiah 6, Hebrews 13	08	Deuteronomy 12, Psalms 97, 98	Isaiah 40, Revelation 10
09	Numbers 17, 18, Psalm 55	Isaiah 7, James 1	09	Deut. 13, 14, Psalms 99-101	Isaiah 41, Revelation 11
10	Numbers 19, Psalms 56, 57	Isaiah 8-9:7, James 2	10	Deuteronomy 15, Psalm 102	Isaiah 42, Revelation 12
11	Numbers 20, Psalms 58, 59	Isa. 9:8-10:4, James 3	11	Deuteronomy 16, Psalm 103	Isaiah 43, Revelation 13
12	Numbers 21, Psalms 60, 61	Isa. 10:5-34, James 4	12	Deuteronomy 17, Psalm 104	Isaiah 44, Revelation 14
13	Numbers 22, Psalms 62, 63	Isaiah 11, 12, James 5	13	Deuteronomy 18, Psalm 105	Isaiah 45, Revelation 15
14	Numbers 23, Psalms 64, 65	Isaiah 13, 1 Peter 1	14	Deuteronomy 19, Psalm 106	Isaiah 46, Revelation 16
15	Numbers 24, Psalms 66, 67	Isaiah 14, 1 Peter 2	15	Deuteronomy 20, Psalm 107	Isaiah 47, Revelation 17
16	Numbers 25, Psalm 68	Isaiah 15, 1 Peter 3	16	Deut. 21, Psalms 108, 109	Isaiah 48, Revelation 18
17	Numbers 26, Psalm 69	Isaiah 16, 1 Peter 4	17	Deut. 22, Psalms 110, 111	Isaiah 49, Revelation 19
18	Numbers 27, Psalms 70, 71	Isaiah 17, 18, 1 Peter 5	18	Deut. 23, Psalms 112, 113	Isaiah 50, Revelation 20
19	Numbers 28, Psalm 72	Isaiah 19, 20, 2 Peter 1	19	Deut. 24, Psalms 114, 115	Isaiah 51, Revelation 21
20	Numbers 29, Psalm 73	Isaiah 21, 2 Peter 2	20	Deuteronomy 25, Psalm 116	Isaiah 52, Revelation 22
21	Numbers 30, Psalm 74	Isaiah 22, 2 Peter 3	21	Deut. 26, Psalms 117, 118	Isaiah 53, Matthew 1
22	Numbers 31, Psalms 75, 76	Isaiah 23, 1 John 1	22	Deut. 27-28:19, Psalm 119:1-24	Isaiah 54, Matthew 2
23	Numbers 32, Psalm 77	Isaiah 24, 1 John 2	23	Deut. 28:20-68, Psalm 119:25-48	Isaiah 55, Matthew 3
24	Numbers 33, Psalm 78:1-37	Isaiah 25, 1 John 3	24	Deut. 29, Psalm 119:49-72	Isaiah 56, Matthew 4
25	Numbers 34, Psalm 78:38-72	Isaiah 26, 1 John 4	25	Deut. 30, Psalm 119:73-96	Isaiah 57, Matthew 5
26	Numbers 35, Psalm 79	Isaiah 27, 1 John 5	26	Deut. 31, Psalm 119:97-120	Isaiah 58, Matthew 6
27	Numbers 36, Psalm 80	Isaiah 28, 2 John 1	27	Deut. 32, Ps. 119:121-144	Isaiah 59, Matthew 7
28	Deuteronomy 1, Psalms 81, 82	Isaiah 29, 3 John 1	28	Deut. 33, 34, Ps. 119:145-176	Isaiah 60, Matthew 8
29	Deuteronomy 2, Psalms 83, 84	Isaiah 30, Jude 1	29	Joshua 1, Psalms 120-122	Isaiah 61, Matthew 9
30	Deuteronomy 3, Psalm 85	Isaiah 31, Revelation 1	30	Joshua 2, Psalms 123-125	Isaiah 62, Matthew 10
31	Deuteronomy 4, Psalms 86, 87	Isaiah 32, Revelation 2			

JULY THRU' AUGUST

JULY			AUGUST		
Date	Morning	Evening	Date	Morning	Evening
01	Joshua 3, Psalms 126-128	Isaiah 63, Matthew 11	01	Judges 15, Acts 19	Jeremiah 28, Mark 14
02	Joshua 4, Psalms 129-131	Isaiah 64, Matthew 12	02	Judges 16, Acts 20	Jeremiah 29, Mark 15
03	Joshua 5-6:5, Psalms 132-134	Isaiah 65, Matthew 13	03	Judges 17, Acts 21	Jeremiah 30, 31, Mark 16
04	Joshua 6:6-27, Psalms 135-136	Isaiah 66, Matthew 14	04	Judges 18, Acts 22	Jeremiah 32, Psalms 1, 2
05	Joshua 7, Psalms 137, 138	Jeremiah 1, Matthew 15	05	Judges 19, Acts 23	Jeremiah 33, Psalms 3, 4
06	Joshua 8, Psalm 139	Jeremiah 2, Matthew 16	06	Judges 20, Acts 24	Jeremiah 34, Psalms 5, 6
07	Joshua 9, Psalms 140, 141	Jeremiah 3, Matthew 17	07	Judges 21, Acts 25	Jeremiah 35, Psalms 7, 8
08	Joshua 10, Psalms 142, 143	Jeremiah 4, Matthew 18	08	Ruth 1, Acts 26	Jeremiah 36, Psalm 9
09	Joshua 11, Psalm 144	Jeremiah 5, Matthew 19	09	Ruth 2, Acts 27	Jeremiah 37, Psalm 10
10	Joshua 12, 13, Psalm 145	Jeremiah 6, Matthew 20	10	Ruth 3, 4, Acts 28	Jeremiah 38, Ps. 11, 12
11	Joshua 14, 15, Psalms 146, 147	Jeremiah 7, Matthew 21	11	1 Samuel 1, Romans 1	Jeremiah 39, Ps. 13, 14
12	Joshua 16, 17, Psalm 148	Jeremiah 8, Matthew 22	12	1 Samuel 2, Romans 2	Jeremiah 40, Ps. 15, 16
13	Joshua 18, 19, Psalms 149, 150	Jeremiah 9, Matthew 23	13	1 Samuel 3, Romans 3	Jeremiah 41, Psalm 17
14	Joshua 20, 21, Acts 1	Jeremiah 10, Matthew 24	14	1 Samuel 4, Romans 4	Jeremiah 42, Psalm 18
15	Joshua 22, Acts 2	Jeremiah 11, Matthew 25	15	1 Samuel 5, 6, Romans 5	Jeremiah 43, Psalm 19
16	Joshua 23, Acts 3	Jeremiah 12, Matthew 26	16	1 Samuel 7, 8, Romans 6	Jeremiah 44, 45, Ps. 20, 21
17	Joshua 24, Acts 4	Jeremiah 13, Matthew 27	17	1 Samuel 9, Romans 7	Jeremiah 46, Psalm 22
18	Judges 1, Acts 5	Jeremiah 14, Matthew 28	18	1 Samuel 10, Romans 8	Jeremiah 47, Ps. 23, 24
19	Judges 2, Acts 6	Jeremiah 15, Mark 1	19	1 Samuel 11, Romans 9	Jeremiah 48, Psalm 25
20	Judges 3, Acts 7	Jeremiah 16, Mark 2	20	1 Samuel 12, Romans 10	Jeremiah 49, Ps. 26, 27
21	Judges 4, Acts 8	Jeremiah 17, Mark 3	21	1 Samuel 13, Romans 11	Jeremiah 50, Ps. 28, 29
22	Judges 5, Acts 9	Jeremiah 18, Mark 4	22	1 Samuel 14, Romans 12	Jeremiah 51, Psalm 30
23	Judges 6, Acts 10	Jeremiah 19, Mark 5	23	1 Samuel 15, Romans 13	Jeremiah 52, Psalm 31
24	Judges 7, Acts 11	Jeremiah 20, Mark 6	24	1 Samuel 16, Romans 14	Lamentations 1, Ps. 32
25	Judges 8, Acts 12	Jeremiah 21, Mark 7	25	1 Samuel 17, Romans 15	Lamentations 2, Ps. 33
26	Judges 9, Acts 13	Jeremiah 22, Mark 8	26	1 Samuel 18, Romans 16	Lamentations 3, Ps. 34
27	Judges 10-11:11, Acts 14	Jeremiah 23, Mark 9	27	1 Samuel 19, 1 Corinthians 1	Lamentations 4, Ps. 35
28	Judges 11:12-40, Acts 15	Jeremiah 24, Mark 10	28	1 Samuel 20, 1 Corinthians 2	Lamentations 5, Ps. 36
29	Judges 12, Acts 16	Jeremiah 25, Mark 11	29	1 Samuel 21, 22, 1 Corinthians 3	Ezekiel 1, Psalm 37
30	Judges 13, Acts 17	Jeremiah 26, Mark 12	30	1 Samuel 23, 1 Corinthians 4	Ezekiel 2, Psalm 38
31	Judges 14, Acts 18	Jeremiah 27, Mark 13	31	1 Samuel 24, 1 Corinthians 5	Ezekiel 3, Psalm 39

SEPTEMBER THRU' OCTOBER

SEPTEMBER			OCTOBER		
Date	Morning	Evening	Date	Morning	Evening
01	1 Samuel 25, 1 Cor. 6	Ezekiel 4, Psalmss 40, 41	01	1 Kings 3, Ephesians 1	Ezekiel 34, Psalms 83, 84
02	1 Samuel 26, 1 Cor. 7	Ezekiel 5, Psalmss 42, 43	02	1 Kings 4, 5, Ephesians 2	Ezekiel 35, Psalms 85
03	1 Samuel 27, 1 Cor. 8	Ezekiel 6, Psalms 44	03	1 Kings 6, Ephesians 3	Ezekiel 36, Psalm 86
04	1 Samuel 28, 1 Cor. 9	Ezekiel 7, Psalms 45	04	1 Kings 7, Ephesians 4	Ezekiel 37, Psalms 87, 88
05	1 Samuel 29, 30, 1 Cor. 10	Ezekiel 8, Psalms 46, 47	05	1 Kings 8, Ephesians 5	Ezekiel 38, Psalm 89
06	1 Samuel 31, 1 Cor. 11	Ezekiel 9, Psalm 48	06	1 Kings 9, Ephesians 6	Ezekiel 39, Psalm 90
07	2 Samuel 1, 1 Cor. 12	Ezekiel 10, Psalm 49	07	1 Kings 10, Philippians 1	Ezekiel 40, Psalm 91
08	2 Samuel 2, 1 Cor. 13	Ezekiel 11, Psalm 50	08	1 Kings 11, Philippians 2	Ezekiel 41, Psalms 92, 93
09	2 Samuel 3, 1 Cor. 14	Ezekiel 12, Psalm 51	09	1 Kings 12, Philippians 3	Ezekiel 42, Psalm 94
10	2 Samuel 4, 5, 1 Cor. 15	Ezekiel 13, Psalms 52-54	10	1 Kings 13, Philippians 4	Ezekiel 43, Psalms 95, 96
11	2 Samuel 6, 1 Cor. 16	Ezekiel 14, Psalm 55	11	1 Kings 14, Colossians 1	Ezekiel 44, Psalms 97, 98
12	2 Samuel 7, 2 Cor. 1	Ezekiel 15, Psalms 56, 57	12	1 Kings 15, Colossians 2	Ezekiel 45, Psalms 99-101
13	2 Samuel 8, 9, 2 Cor. 2	Ezekiel 16, Psalms 58, 59	13	1 Kings 16, Colossians 3	Ezekiel 46, Psalm 102
14	2 Samuel 10, 2 Cor. 3	Ezekiel 17, Psalms 60, 61	14	1 Kings 17, Colossians 4	Ezekiel 47, Psalms 103
15	2 Samuel 11, 2 Cor. 4	Ezekiel 18, Psalms 62, 63	15	1 Kings 18, 1 Thess. 1	Ezekiel 48, Psalm 104
16	2 Samuel 12, 2 Cor. 5	Ezekiel 19, Psalms 64, 65	16	1 Kings 19, 1 Thess. 2	Daniel 1, Psalm 105
17	2 Samuel 13, 2 Cor. 6	Ezekiel 20, Psalms 66, 67	17	1 Kings 20, 1 Thess. 3	Daniel 2, Psalm 106
18	2 Samuel 14, 2 Cor. 7	Ezekiel 21, Psalm 68	18	1 Kings 21, 1 Thess. 4	Daniel 3, Psalm 107
19	2 Samuel 15, 2 Cor. 8	Ezekiel 22, Psalm 69	19	1 Kings 22, 1 Thess. 5	Daniel 4, Psalms 108, 109
20	2 Samuel 16, 2 Cor. 9	Ezekiel 23, Psalms 70, 71	20	2 Kings 1, 2 Thess. 1	Daniel 5, Psalms 110, 111
21	2 Samuel 17, 2 Cor. 10	Ezekiel 24, Psalm 72	21	2 Kings 2, 2 Thess. 2	Daniel 6, Psalms 112, 113
22	2 Samuel 18, 2 Cor. 11	Ezekiel 25, Psalm 73	22	2 Kings 3, 2 Thess. 3	Daniel 7, Psalms 114, 115
23	2 Samuel 19, 2 Cor. 12	Ezekiel 26, Psalm 74	23	2 Kings 4, 1 Timothy 1	Daniel 8, Psalm 116
24	2 Samuel 20, 2 Cor. 13	Ezekiel 27, Psalms 75, 76	24	2 Kings 5, 1 Timothy 2	Daniel 9, Psalms 117, 118
25	2 Samuel 21, Galatians 1	Ezekiel 28, Psalm 77	25	2 Kings 6, 1 Timothy 3	Daniel 10, Psalm 119:1-24
26	2 Samuel 22, Galatians 2	Ezekiel 29, Psalm 78:1-37	26	2 Kings 7, 1 Timothy 4	Daniel 11, Psalm 119:25-48
27	2 Samuel 23, Galatians 3	Ezekiel 30, Psalm 78:38-72	27	2 Kings 8, 1 Timothy 5	Daniel 12, Psalm 119:49-72
28	2 Samuel 24, Galatians 4	Ezekiel 31, Psalm 79	28	2 Kings 9, 1 Timothy 6	Hosea 1, Psalm 119:73-96
29	1 Kings 1, Galatians 5	Ezekiel 32, Psalm 80	29	2 Kings 10, 11, 2 Timothy 1	Hosea 2, Psalm 119:97-120
30	1 Kings 2, Galatians 6	Ezekiel 33, Psalms 81, 82	30	2 Kings 12, 2 Timothy 2	Hosea 3, 4, Psalm 119:121-144
			31	2 Kings 13, 2 Timothy 3	Hosea 5, 6, Psalm 119:145-176

NOVEMBER THRU' DECEMBER

NOVEMBER			DECEMBER		
Date	Morning	Evening	Date	Morning	Evening
01	2 Kings 14, 2, Timothy 4	Hosea 7, Ps. 120-122	01	1 Chronicles 29, 2 Peter 3	Micah 6, Luke 15
02	2 Kings 15, Titus 1	Hosea 8, Ps. 123-125	02	2 Chronicles 1, 1 John 1	Micah 7, Luke 16
03	2 Kings 16, Titus 2	Hosea 9, Ps. 126-128	03	2 Chronicles 2, 1 John 2	Nahum 1, Luke 17
04	2 Kings 17, Titus 3	Hosea 10, Ps. 129-131	04	2 Chronicles 3, 4, 1 John 3	Nahum 2, Luke 18
05	2 Kings 18, Philemon	Hosea 11, Ps. 132-134	05	2 Chron. 5-6:11, 1 John 4	Nahum 3, Luke 19
06	2 Kings 19, Hebrews 1	Hosea 12, Ps. 135, 136	06	2 Chron. 6:12-42, 1 John 5	Habakkuk 1, Luke 20
07	2 Kings 20, Hebrews 2	Hosea 13, Ps. 137, 138	07	2 Chronicles 7, 2 John 1	Habakkuk 2, Luke 21
08	2 Kings 21, Hebrews 3	Hosea 14, Ps. 139	08	2 Chronicles 8, 3 John 1	Habakkuk 3, Luke 22
09	2 Kings 22, Hebrews 4	Joel 1, Psalms 140, 141	09	2 Chronicles 9, Jude 1	Zephaniah 1, Luke 23
10	2 Kings 23, Hebrews 5	Joel 2, Psalm 142	10	2 Chronicles 10, Rev. 1	Zephaniah 2, Luke 24
11	2 Kings 24, Hebrews 6	Joel 3, Psalm 143	11	2 Chronicles 11, 12, Rev. 2	Zephaniah 3, John 1
12	2 Kings 25, Hebrews 7	Amos 1, Psalm 144	12	2 Chronicles 13, Rev. 3	Haggai 1, John 2
13	1 Chronicles 1, 2, Heb. 8	Amos 2, Psalm 145	13	2 Chronicles 14, 15, Rev. 4	Haggai 2, John 3
14	1 Chronicles 3, 4, Heb. 9	Amos 3, Psalms 146, 147	14	2 Chronicles 16, Rev. 5	Zechariah 1, John 4
15	1 Chronicles 5, 6, Heb. 10	Amos 4, Psalms 148-150	15	2 Chronicles 17, Rev. 6	Zechariah 2, John 5
16	1 Chronicles 7, 8, Heb. 11	Amos 5, Luke 1:1-38	16	2 Chronicles 18, Rev. 7	Zechariah 3, John 6
17	1 Chronicles 9, 10, Heb. 12	Amos 6, Luke 1:39-80	17	2 Chronicles 19, 20, Rev. 8	Zechariah 4, John 7
18	1 Chronicles 11, 12, Heb. 13	Amos 7, Luke 2	18	2 Chronicles 21, Rev. 9	Zechariah 5, John 8
19	1 Chronicles 13, 14, James 1	Amos 8, Luke 3	19	2 Chron. 22, 23, Rev. 10	Zechariah 6, John 9
20	1 Chronicles 15, James 2	Amos 9, Luke 4	20	2 Chronicles 24, Rev. 11	Zechariah 7, John 10
21	1 Chronicles 16, James 3	Obadiah, Luke 5	21	2 Chronicles 25, Rev. 12	Zechariah 8, John 11
22	1 Chronicles 17, James 4	Jonah 1, Luke 6	22	2 Chronicles 26, Rev. 13	Zechariah 9, John 12
23	1 Chronicles 18, James 5	Jonah 2, Luke 7	23	2 Chron. 27, 28, Rev. 14	Zechariah 10, John 13
24	1 Chronicles 19, 20, 1 Peter 1	Jonah 3, Luke 8	24	2 Chronicles 29, Rev. 15	Zechariah 11, John 14
25	1 Chronicles 21, 1 Peter 2	Jonah 4, Luke 9	25	2 Chronicles 30, Rev. 16	Zechariah 12-13:1, John 15
26	1 Chronicles 22, 1 Peter 3	Micah 1, Luke 10	26	2 Chronicles 31, Rev. 17	Zechariah 13:2-9, John 16
27	1 Chronicles 23, 1 Peter 4	Micah 2, Luke 11	27	2 Chronicles 32, Rev. 18	Zechariah 14, John 17
28	1 Chronicles 24, 25, 1 Peter 5	Micah 3, Luke 12	28	2 Chronicles 33, Rev. 19	Malachi 1, John 18
29	1 Chronicles 26, 27, 2 Peter 1	Micah 4, Luke 13	29	2 Chronicles 34, Rev. 20	Malachi 2, John 19
30	1 Chronicles 28, 2 Peter 2	Micah 5, Luke 14	30	2 Chronicles 35, Rev. 21	Malachi 3, John 20
			31	2 Chronicles 36, Rev. 22	Malachi 4, John 21

Methods of Bible study

R. A. Torrey

Reuben Archer Torrey, 1856-1928, educator, pastor, world evangelist and author, was appointed by D. L. Moody as the first head of what became known as the Moody Bible Institute. He wrote the book *Methods of Bible Study* from which the following studies have been edited.

Getting started

1. Every day

First of all make up your mind that you will *put some time — every day — into the study of the Word of God*. Nothing short of illness should be allowed to interfere with this daily study.

2. How long?

I know many busy people who give an hour a day to Bible study, but if one cannot give more than 15 minutes a day a great deal can still be accomplished.

3. Study

Make up your mind to study the Bible. The Bible is good only because of the truth that is in it, and to see this truth demands close attention. One must look for a long time at the great masterpieces of art to appreciate their beauty and understand their meaning, and so one must look for a long time at the great verses of the Bible to appreciate their beauty and understand their meaning.

4. Questions to ask

When you read a verse in the Bible ask yourself:

   a. What does this verse mean?
   b. Then ask: What does it mean for me?
   c. Then ask: Is that all it means?

5. Study topically

Study the Bible topically.

It is important to know all that God has to say. Many people know part of what God has to say — and usually a very small part — and so their ideas are very imperfect and one-sided. The only way to know all God has to say on any subject is to go through the Bible studying that subject. Make use of a Bible concordance here.

6. For example

To study "Prayer" look up in your concordance the passages that contain the words "pray," "prayer," "cry," "ask," "call," "supplication," "intercession," etc. When you have gone through them you will know far more about prayer than you ever knew before.

Topical study of the Bible

1. Be systematic

Have a carefully prepared list of the subjects you need to know about, and study them one by one.

2. Be thorough

As you study a topic do not be content to look up just a few passages but look up every passage in the Bible on this subject.

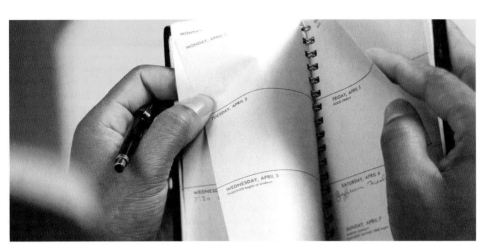

3. Be exact

First, note the exact words used.

Second, discover the exact meaning of the words used. Do this by finding how the word is used in the Bible. The Bible's use of some words differs from the way we understand these words today. The Bible words "sanctification" and "justification" are two examples of this.

Third, note the preceding verse and following verse to the one you are studying. This will often shed light on the meaning of a verse.

Fourth, see if there are any parallel passages. The meaning of many of the most difficult passages in the Bible is made perfectly plain by some other passages that throw light on them.

4. Write down your results

Take the example of the subject of "Prayer" again.

If you decided to make your own classification of the Bible verses you have looked up, you might list them under the following headings:

- What prayers does God listen to?
- To whom should we pray?
- For whom should we pray?
- When to pray?
- Where to pray?
- What should we pray for?
- How to pray.
- Hindrances to prayer.
- The results of prayer.

Important topics to study

Here is a list of some subjects that every Christian should study and study as soon as possible.

- The Atonement (of the blood of Christ; the death of Christ)
- Justification
- The new birth
- Adoption
- Sanctification
- Holiness
- Assurance

- The flesh
- Faith
- Prayer
- Praise
- Love:
     To God, To Jesus Christ
     To Christians, To all men
- The future destiny of believers
- The future destiny of the wicked:
     Punishment of the wicked
     Death of the wicked
- The character of Christ
- The resurrection of Christ
- The ascension of Christ
- The second coming of Christ:
     The fact, The manner
     The purpose, The results
     The time, The reign of Christ
- The Holy Spirit:
     Who he is, His work
- God:
     His attributes, His work
- Grace
- Messianic prophecies
- The church
- Joy
- Life
- Perfection

- Cleansing
- Repentance
- Thanksgiving
- Sin

- The Jews
- The judgment
- Peace
- Persecution

Examples of Bible study
Study the Bible by chapters
This method of Bible study is not beyond anyone who has 15 minutes a day to put into Bible Study. It will take, however, more than one day to study a chapter if only 15 minutes a day are set apart for the work.

A. Select the chapters you wish to study.

It is best to take a whole book and study the chapters in order. The Acts of the Apostles is a good book to begin with.

B. Read the chapter for today's study five times.

It is good to read it aloud at least once. Each new reading will bring out some new point.

C. Divide the chapters into their natural divisions and find striking headings which describe their contents.

For example, suppose you are studying 1 John chapter 5. You might divide it up like this:

- vs 1-3 The believer's noble parentage
- vs 4, 5 The believer's glorious victory
- vs 6-10 The believer's sure ground of faith
- vs 11, 12 The believer's priceless possession
- v 13 The believer's blessed assurance
- vs 14, 15 The believer's unquestioning confidence
- vs 16, 17 The believer's great power and responsibility
- vs 18, 19 The believer's perfect security
- v 20 The believer's precious knowledge
- v 21 The believer's constant duty

D. Note the important differences between the best modern Bible translations and the *King James Version*.

E. Write down the main facts of the chapter in order.

F. Make a note of the people mentioned in the chapter and of any light thrown on their character.

For example, if the chapter you are studying is Acts chapter 16, then the people mentioned are:

- Timothy
- Timothy's mother
- Timothy's father
- The brethren at Lystra and Iconium
- Paul
- The Jews of Lystra and Iconium
- The apostles and elders at Jerusalem
- A man of Macedonia
- Luke
- Some women of Philippi
- Lydia
- The household of Lydia
- A slave girl possessed with a spirit of divination
- The owners of this slave girl
- Silas
- The magistrates of Philippi
- The Philippian mob
- The Philippian jailor
- The prisoners in the Philippian jail
- The household of the jailor
- The officers of Philippi
- The Christians in Philippi

What light does the chapter throw upon the character of each?

G. Note the principal lessons of the chapter. Classify these as follows:

   i. lessons about God
  ii. lessons about Christ
 iii. lessons about the Holy Spirit, etc.

H. The central truth of the chapter.

I. The key verse of the chapter if there is one.

J. The best verse in the chapter. Opinions will differ widely here. But the question is, which is the best verse to you as you have read the chapter? Mark it and memorize it.

K. Give a heading to each chapter. For example:

Acts 1: The Ascension
Acts 2: The Day of Pentecost
Acts 3: The lame man

L. Note subjects for further study. For example, from your study of Acts 1, subjects suggested for further study are:

The Baptism with the Holy Spirit; The Ascension; The second coming of Christ.

M. Note words and phrases for further study. For example, from studying John's Gospel, chapter 3, you should look up words and expressions such as:

- Eternal life
- Born again
- Water
- Believer
- The Kingdom of God

N. Write down what new truth you have learned from the chapter.

O. What truth already known has come to you with new power?

P. What definite thing have you resolved to do as a result of studying this chapter? A permanent record should be kept of the results of the study of each chapter.

Study the Bible as the Word of God

The Bible is the Word of God. It is often said that we should study the Bible just as we study any other book. That principle contains a truth, but it also contains a great error. The Bible, it is true, is a book as other books are books; the laws of grammatical and literary construction and interpretation are the same here as in any other book. But the

Bible is a unique book. It is what no other book is — the Word of God. So the Bible should be studied like no other book. It should be studied as the Word of God (1 Thessalonians 2:13).

1. We must study this book very carefully so that we can discover the mind of God which it reveals.
2. We must accept its teachings.
3. We must rely on all its promises.
4. As we study the Bible we remember that we are in God's presence and that he will speak to us.
5. Study the Bible prayerfully.
6. Look for "the things concerning Christ" "in all the Scriptures." Christ is everywhere in the Bible (Luke 24:27).
7. Store away the Scripture in your mind and heart. It will:
   - keep you from sin (Psalm 119:11 *RV*)
   - keep you from false doctrine (Acts 20:29, 30, 32; 2 Timothy 3:13-15)
   - fill your heart with joy (Jeremiah 15:16) and peace (Psalm 85:8)
   - give you the victory over the Evil One (1 John 2:14)
   - give you power in prayer (John 15:7)
   - make you wise (Psalm 119:98, 100, 130)
   - make you "thoroughly equipped for every good work" (2 Timothy 3:16-17).

Basic tips about Bible study

THE PROTESTANT OLD TESTAMENT	
What to do	*What to avoid*
1. Have a regular, private place for your study.	Being upset when you miss your time.
2. Pray before you start. • Pray in a spirit of humility. • Ask God to direct your mind as you study.	Let the word of God correct you, rather than you correcting God!
3. Start with what you know. Use these scriptures to understand harder, vaguer passages of God's word.	Do not build doctrine on one scripture!
4. Let the Bible interpret and prove the Bible.	Don't look for what you want to prove; look for what the Bible says.
5. Understand the context of the verses you read. Look at the verses before and after, as well as the chapters before and after.	Avoid thinking that the Bible contradicts itself.
6. Ask questions: • What is the straightforward meaning? • What does the scripture not say? • What do the verses teach about God? • What do the verses teach about Jesus? • What do the verses teach about the Holy Spirit? • Is there any command for me to obey? • Is there a warning for me to heed? • Is there a promise for me to claim?	Avoid relying on your own personal ideas and preconceived notions.
7. Pray as you end. • Thank God for what he has taught you. • Ask for his grace to put into practice what you have read.	Avoid being a listener only.

Bible markings: how can marking my bible and using symbols help me?

Bible markings

Some people have great misgivings about making any marks on their Bible. However, making marks on a Bible is one way to preserve the labors of hours of Bible study and can remind us about how a particular verse or truth has helped us in the past.

The simplest of marks
Circling

This is the simplest kind of mark to make. It helps to highlight a verse which has especially struck you.

Underscoring

This has the same effect as circling, but makes the verse stand out even more.

> For God so loved the world that
> he gave his one and only Son,
> that whoever believes in him shall
> not perish but have eternal life.
> *John 3:16*

Using a felt-tip pen to shade in the whole verse is another way of doing this.

Just making a line in the margin next to the verse is an alternative method.

USING COLORS	
Underscoring or circling with a color enables you to emphasize different things. Choose a color that has a symbolic meaning for you. Once you have chosen a color stick to it.	
YELLOW	
Promises	Every time you come across a promise in the Bible you can mark it in yellow.
PURPLE	
Kingship	Bible verses about God's majesty and Jesus kingship can be marked in purple.
RED	
Jesus' death	Red is the color of blood and can be used to note passages about Jesus' death. NB: In the New Testament the "blood" of Jesus always stands for the "death" of Jesus. *"But if we walk in the light, as he is in the light, we have fellowship with one another, and the blood of Jesus, his Son, purifies us from all sin." 1 John 1:7*
GREEN	
Future hope	Green is for evergreen and stand for anything that refers to hope and the future. *"For the perishable must clothe itself with the imperishable, and the mortal with immortality." 1 Corinthians 15:53*

BIBLE STUDY MADE SIMPLE

21

BIBLE MARKINGS: HOW CAN MARKING MY BIBLE AND USING SYMBOLS HELP ME?

Dates

Some people put in the date on which a Bible verse or Bible passage has especially spoken to them. Next to the date a name or event can be written to remind us about the significance of the verse. *9/9/01 John went into hospital*

Symbols

Symbols can be drawn in the margin of the Bible opposite the relevant verse.

- The symbol of the cross can stand for Jesus' sacrifice.
- The symbol of a heart can stand for God's love.
- The symbol of musical notes can stand for something to praise God for.
- The symbol of an open book can stand for the Word of God.
- The symbol of a smiling face could be used for verses about God's comfort

You can make up a list of symbols for your own use.

Symbols and letters

Symbols are best used to represent key Bible themes.

You can divide these themes up in the following way.

If, for example, you chose to use the symbol of a dove for the Holy Spirit, you could write a letter on the dove to stand for different aspects of the Holy Spirit's ministry:

I in the dove could stand for the Holy Spirit *indwelling* us. An appropriate verse for this would be, 1 Corinthians 3:16, "Don't you know that you yourselves are God's temple and that God's Spirit lives in you?"

T The letter **T** could stand for *teaching* about the Holy Spirit, and so on.

Letters are best used to denote a particular aspect of a topic.

Studying a single Bible verse: the microscopic approach

THE "GREATEST" VERSE IN THE BIBLE	
Here are 12 reasons why this verse is so highly rated by Christians, especially by evangelists.	
Word/s from verse	Deduction
1. God	God is the greatest Lover
2. So loved	God loved to the greatest possible degree
3. The world	God loved the greatest number of people
4. That he gave	God's greatest act was giving Jesus
5. His one and only Son	Jesus is the greatest gift in the world
6. That whoever	This is humankind's greatest opportunity
7. Believes	The greatest, yet simplest step
8. In him	Jesus is the greatest attraction in the world
9. Shall not perish	This is God's greatest promise
10. But	This is the greatest difference
11. Have	This is the greatest certainty
12. Eternal life	This is the greatest possession

John 3:16

John chapter 3, verse 16 has been called the greatest sentence in the English language.

"For God so loved the world that he gave his one and only Son, that whoever believes in him shall not perish but have eternal life."

Unpacking John 3:16

For God – God is the Lord of heaven and earth

so loved – God loved the world so much that he longed for the world to be forgiven

the world – the world that is full of sin and rebellion against God

that he gave – Jesus was the most costly gift God could bestow on us

his one and only Son – God sent Jesus to take our place on the cross

that whoever – God's grace extends to everyone

believes – this is simply placing one's trust in Jesus

in him – that is trusting the righteous and just One

shall not perish – in their sin

but have eternal life – which is given to us by Jesus.

God's answer to

In John 3:16 certain basic answers about belief in God are given.

1. *atheism*: John 3:16 affirms that God does exist. The verse starts with the word: "God."
2. *agnosticism*: John 3:16 states that this is who God is like: "God so loved."
3. *skepticism*: John 3:16 proclaims with total assurance that the believer: "shall not perish but have eternal life."
4. *legalism*: John 3:16 says that it is the "believer" who will have eternal life.

Ask questions

One of the most fruitful ways to study a Bible verse is to ask questions about it.

Question 1: What does this verse teach about God?

A. *God the Father*
   It is out of love that God the Father sent Jesus to the world.
B. *God the Son*
   God the Son came that we might have eternal life.

Question 2: Is there any promise in this verse to appropriate?

If we believe in Jesus we are given the gift of eternal life.

Question 3: Is there any warning in this verse?

This verse states that those who refuse to believe will "perish."

Question 4: Is there a command to obey in this verse, or does it tell me to do something?

It is implicit in John 3:16 that we are meant to believe in Jesus.

Using John 3:16 as a springboard

There are a number of topics in John 3:16 which are expanded in other Bible verses.

1. Love

John's Gospel often speaks about love:

- People *love* darkness, 3:19
- God the Father *loves* his Son, 3:35; 5:20
- Some people have no *love* for God in their hearts, 5:41
- Anyone who has God as their Father will *love* Jesus, 8:42
- God the Father *loves* Jesus because he was willing to give up his life, 10:17
- Jesus *loved* Martha, Mary and Lazarus, 11:5
- Anyone who *loves* his own life will lose it, 12:25
- Jesus *loved* his disciples to the end, even though they were to desert him, 13:1
- Jesus' new commandment is that we should *love* one another, 13:34
- We are *loved* by Jesus as much as the Father loves Jesus, 15:9
- Jesus said that the Father himself *loves* us because we love and trust Jesus, 16:27

Studying a particular word from the Bible

Gentleness

1. Gentleness is a characteristic of God

He tends his flock like a shepherd:
  he gathers the lambs in his arms
and carries them close to his heart;
  he **gently** leads those that have
young. *Isaiah 40:11*

2. God sometimes communicates in a gentle way

After the earthquake came a fire, but the LORD was not in the fire. And after the fire came a **gentle** whisper. *1 Kings 19:12*

3. How to cool tempers

A **gentle** answer turns away wrath, but a harsh word stirs up anger. *Proverbs 15:1*

4. Gentleness is effective

Through patience a ruler can be persuaded, and a **gentle** tongue can break a bone. *Proverbs 25:15*

5. Jesus and his gentle approach

Rejoice greatly, O Daughter of Zion! Shout, Daughter of Jerusalem! See, your king comes to you, righteous and having salvation, **gentle** and riding on a donkey, on a colt, the foal of a donkey. *Zechariah 9:9*

  "Say to the Daughter of Zion,
'See, your king comes to you,
gentle and riding on a donkey,
on a colt, the foal of a donkey.'"
Matthew 21:5

6. Jesus is gentle

Take my yoke upon you and learn from me, for I am **gentle** and humble in heart, and you will find rest for your souls. *Matthew 11:29*

7. A whip or a gentle spirit?

Paul told off the Corinthian Christians in his first letter to them and so asked them, "What do you prefer? Shall I come to you with a whip, or in love and with a **gentle** spirit?" *1 Corinthians 4:21*

8. Making appeal to Jesus' gentleness

By the meekness and **gentleness** of Christ, I appeal to you—I, Paul, who am "timid" when face to face with you, but "bold" when away! *2 Corinthians 10:1*

9. Gentleness and the fruit of the spirit

...**gentleness** and self-control. Against such things there is no law. *Galatians 5:23*

  This list of nine things in Galatians 5:23, are sometimes called the fruits, in the plural, of the Spirit. Strictly speaking they all make up the fruit, in the singular, of the Spirit.

  Another way to look at this is to think of "love" as the fruit of the Spirit, as all the other eight qualities are varities of love:

- Joy is love singing
- Peace is love resting
- Patience is love enduring
- Kindness is love's touch

- Goodness is love's character
- Faithfulness is love's habit
- Gentleness is love's self-denial
- Self-control is love in charge

10. A command to be gentle
Be completely humble and **gentle**; be patient, bearing with one another in love. *Ephesians 4:2*

11. Gentleness is to be displayed
Let your **gentleness** be evident to all. The Lord is near. *Philippians 4:5*

12. Gentleness linked with patience
Therefore, as God's chosen people, holy and dearly loved, clothe yourselves with compassion, kindness, humility, **gentleness** and patience. *Colossians 3:12*

13. Paul was like a gentle mother
...but we were **gentle** among you, like a mother caring for her little children...as a father...with his own children. *1 Thessalonians 2:7, 10*

14. One of the qualifications for an overseer
...not given to drunkenness, not violent but **gentle**, not quarrelsome, not a lover of money. *1 Timothy 3:3*

15. Required in a godly person
But you, man of God, flee from all this, and pursue righteousness, godliness, faith, love, endurance and **gentleness**. *1 Timothy 6:11*

16. Inner beauty
Instead, it should be that of your inner self, the unfading beauty of a **gentle** and quiet spirit, which is of great worth in God's sight. *1 Peter 3:4*

17. How to witness
But in your hearts set apart Christ as Lord. Always be prepared to give an answer to everyone who asks you to give the reason for the hope that you have. But do this with **gentleness** and respect... *1 Peter 3:15*

Basic facts to remember about the Bible

Why God gave us the Scriptures

The more we remember that the Bible is inspired by God and given by him for our benefit the more likely we are to read the Bible and treasure what it says.

What the Bible itself says it will do for us as we read it

It makes us wise about salvation

"…from infancy you have known the holy scriptures, which are able *to make you wise for salvation* through faith in Christ Jesus." *2 Timothy 3:15*

It illumines us

"Your word is a lamp to my feet and a light to my path." *Psalm 119:105*

It enables us to follow God's ways

"It [God's law] is to be with him, and he

is to read it all the days of his life so that he may learn to revere the Lord his God and follow carefully all the words of this law and these decrees."
Deuteronomy 17:19

It equips us to defeat Satan's attacks

"Put on the full armor of God so that you can take your stand against the devil's schemes…Take the helmet of salvation and the sword of the Spirit, which is the word of God."
Ephesians 6:11, 17

It helps to make us holy

"Sanctify them by the truth; your word is truth." *John 17:17*

It helps us not to sin

"I have hidden your word in my heart that I might not sin against you."
Psalm 119:11

It helps us in our worship and as we teach others about Jesus

"Let the word of Christ dwell in you richly as you teach and admonish one another with all wisdom, and as you sing psalms, hymns and spiritual songs with gratitude in your hearts to God."
Colossians 3:16

It enables us to grow spiritually

"Like newborn babies, crave pure spiritual milk, so that by it you may grow up in your salvation, now that you have tasted that the Lord is good."
1 Peter 2:2

Studying a large section of the Bible: the telescopic approach

Summaries

There are a number of places in the Bible which give summaries of other long and extended passages of the Bible.

Before Stephen, the first Christian martyr, was stoned he gave a speech to the Jewish Council, the Sanhedrin, which is recorded in Acts 7:1-50. It gives a comprehensive summary of the history of the Old Testament, from Abraham to Solomon.

For anybody unfamiliar with the Old Testament, or for anyone who wants to study it afresh, you could start by reading Acts 7:1-50. Then read the verses from this passage in conjunction with the passages they refer to in the Old Testament.

SUMMARIES		
Theme	*Acts 7:1-50*	*Old Testament*
Abraham in Mesopotamia	verse 2	Genesis 11:31, 32
The call of Abraham	verses 2-5	Genesis 12:1-5
An inheritance is promised	verses 6, 7	Genesis 12:6, 7
The covenant of circumcision	verse 8a	Genesis 17:9-14
Jacob and the 12 patriarchs	verse 8b	Genesis 29:31-35; 30:5-13, 17-24
Brothers jealous of Joseph	verse 9	Genesis 37:1-4, 12-36
Joseph made ruler of Egypt	verse 10	Genesis 41:39-43
Famine in Egypt	verse 11	Genesis 41:54-57
Jacob hears about grain in Egypt	verse 12	Genesis 42:1, 2
Joseph makes himself known	verse 13	Genesis 45:1-4
Joseph sends for his family	verse 14	Genesis 45:9, 10
Jacob goes to Egypt	verse 15	Genesis 46:5-7
Jacob buried in Canaan	verse 16	Genesis 50:13
Israelites increase greatly in Egypt	verse 17	Exodus 1:7
A new ruler in Egypt	verse 18	Exodus 1:8
Israelites dealt with harshly	verse 19	Exodus 1:10-22
Birth of Moses	verse 20	Exodus 2:2
Pharaoh's daughter brings up Moses	verse 21	Exodus 2:3-10
Moses educated	verse 22	1 Kings 4:30; Isaiah 19:11
Moses visits his fellow-Israelites	verses 23-28	Exodus 2:11-14
Moses flees to Midian	verse 29	Exodus 2:15
Moses and the burning bush	verses 30-32	Exodus 3:1-4
"Take off your sandals"	verses 33, 34	Exodus 3:5-10
Moses delivers the Israelites	verses 35, 36	Exodus 12:41
Moses the prophet	verse 37	Deuteronomy 18:18
Moses on Mount Sinai	verse 38	Exodus 19:17
Aaron and the golden calf	verses 39-43	Numbers 14:3, 4; Exodus 32:1-6
The tabernacle of the Testimony	verse 44	Exodus 38:21
Joshua and the tabernacle	verse 45	Joshua 3:14-17
David	verse 46	2 Samuel 8:7-16
Solomon builds the temple	verses 47-50	1 Kings 6:1-38

Linking up the Old Testament with the New Testament

Fulfilled prophecies

Another way to have a telescopic view of the whole Bible is to study a doctrine that runs through the Bible, from Genesis to Revelation.

One such topic is the prophecies in the Old Testament about Jesus which the Old Testament says have been fulfilled. (All the Bible references on this topic are from the *King James Version*.)

FULFILLED PROPHECIES		
Prophetic scripture	*Topic*	*Fulfilled in Jesus*
"And I will put enmity between you and the woman, and between your seed and her seed. He shall bruise your head, and you shall bruise His heel." *Genesis 3:15*	Seed of a woman	"But when the fulness of the time had come, God sent forth His Son, born of a woman, born under the law." *Galatians 4:4*
"Of the increase of His govern-ment and peace there will be no end, upon the throne of David and over His kingdom, to order it and establish it with judgment and justice from that time forward, even forever." *Isaiah 9:7*	Heir to David's throne	"He will be great, and will be called the Son of the Highest; and the Lord God will give Him the throne of His father David. And He will reign over the house of Jacob forever, and of His kingdom there will be no end." *Luke 1:32, 33*
JESUS' BIRTH AND CHILDHOOD		
"But you, Bethlehem, Ephrathah, though you are little among the thousands of Judah, yet out of you shall come forth to Me the One to be ruler in Israel…" *Micah 5:2*	Born in Bethlehem	"And Joseph also went up from Galilee, out of the city of Nazareth, into Judea, to the city of David, which is called Bethlehem, because he was of the house and lineage of David, to be registered with Mary, his betrothed wife, who was with child." *Luke 2:4, 5*
"Therefore the Lord Himself will give you a sign, Behold, the virgin shall conceive and bear a Son, and shall call His name Immanuel." *Isaiah 7:14*	To be born of a virgin	"Now in the sixth month the angel Gabriel was sent by God to a city of Galilee named Nazareth, to a virgin betrothed to a man whose name was Joseph, of the house of David. The virgin's name was Mary." *Luke 1:26, 27*

"Thus says the Lord: 'A voice was heard in Ramah, lamentation and bitter weeping, Rachel weeping for her children, refusing to be comforted for her children, because they are no more.'" *Jeremiah 31:15*	Slaughter of children	"Then Herod, when he saw that he was deceived by the wise men, was exceeding angry; and he sent forth and put to death all the male children who were in Bethlehem and in all its districts, from two years old and under, according to the time which he had determined from the wise men. Then was fulfilled what was spoken by Jeremiah the prophet, saying: 'A voice was heard in Ramah, lamentation, weeping, and great mourning, Rachel weeping for her children, refusing to be comforted, because they were no more.'" *Matthew 2:16-18*
"When Israel was a child, I loved him, and out of Egypt I called My son." *Hosea 11:1*	Flight to Egypt	"When he arose, he took the young Child and His mother by night and departed for Egypt, and was there until the death of Herod, that it might be fulfilled which was spoken by the Lord through the prophet, saying, 'Out of Egypt I called My Son.'" *Matthew 2:14, 15*
JESUS' PUBLIC MINISTRY		
"The Spirit of the Lord God is upon me, because the Lord has anointed me to preach good tidings to the poor; He has sent me to heal the broken-hearted, to proclaim liberty to the captives, and the opening of the prison to those who are bound; to proclaim the acceptable year of the Lord, and the day of vengeance of our God; to comfort all who mourn." *Isaiah 61:1, 2*	To bind up the broken-hearted	"The Spirit of the Lord God is upon me, because He has anointed me to preach the gospel to the poor: He has sent me to heal the broken-hearted, to preach deliverance to the captives and recovery of sight to the blind, to set at liberty those who are oppressed, to preach the acceptable year of the Lord." *Luke 4:18, 19*

JESUS' LAST WEEK AND PASSION		
"Rejoice greatly, O daughter of Zion! Shout O daughter of Jerusalem! Behold, your King is coming to you: He is just and having salvation, lowly and riding on a donkey, a colt, the foal of a donkey." *Zechariah 9:9*	Entering Jerusalem in triumph	"Then they brought the colt to Jesus and threw their garments on it, and He sat on it…Then those who went before and those who followed cried out, saying: 'Hosanna! Blessed is He who comes in the name of the Lord!'" *Mark 11:7, 9*
"Even my own family friend in whom I trusted, who ate my bread, has lifted up his heel against me." *Psalm 41:9*	Betrayed by a close friend	"He who was called Judas, one of the twelve, went before them and drew near to Jesus to kiss Him. But Jesus said to him, 'Judas, are you betraying the Son of Man with a kiss?'" *Luke 22:47, 48*
"He poured out his soul unto death, and He was numbered with the transgressors, and He bore the sin of many, and made intercession for the transgressors." *Isaiah 53:12*	Killed with thieves	"With Him they also crucified two robbers, one on His right and the other on His left. So the Scripture was fulfilled which says, 'And he was numbered with the transgressors.'" *Mark 15:27, 28*
"…then they will look on me whom they have pierced; they will mourn for him…" *Zechariah 12:10*	Pierced in his death	"But one of the soldiers pierced His side with a spear, and immediately blood and water came out." *John 19:34*

Fulfilled prophecy

Taken together the prophecies about Jesus in the Old Testament are amazing in their accuracy. They were not merely fulfilled in a symbolic way but literally in history.

It was predicted that Jesus would:

- come from David's line
- be born of a virgin
- be born in Bethlehem
- be forced to flee to Egypt
- have a compassionate and healing ministry
- enter Jerusalem in triumph on a donkey
- be betrayed by a friend
- be killed with robbers and be pierced.

Hermeneutics: principles in interpreting the Bible

Pitfalls to avoid

1. People do twist what the Bible says

Peter warned about this in 2 Peter 3:16 where he says that some people were already distorting Paul's letters. Peter did not think that this was a light matter as he goes on to say that this way leads to destruction.

In passing it is worth noting that even Peter says in this verse that Paul writes some things in his letter which are hard to understand!

2. Don't get hung up by anthropomorphisms

In the Bible God speaks in human terms. He condescends to come down to our level. So the Bible frequently uses anthropomorphic language, when God's eternal truth is expressed in human terms.

The word anthropomorphic is derived from two Greek words: *anthropos*, man, and *morphe*, form. So the word means ascribing human form or attributes to beings or things that are not human. So when we read "God repented" or "relented" in Exodus 32:14, or that God "came down" in Exodus 3:8, we find the sense easy to grasp and know that the writer was making use of anthropomorphic language.

Look for the author's meaning

Ask yourself the question, "What did Amos mean when he wrote this warning?" The original writers knew what they were writing about, so try to find out what they meant when they originally put pen to paper.

a. What was going on when the author was writing?

It helps to know who wrote the Bible book we are studying, when he wrote it, to whom he wrote it, why he wrote it. For example, Paul's letter to the Philippians will mean more to us if we recall that he wrote it while he was under house arrest in Rome, and that three of his readers would be a successful business woman – Lydia, a jailor and a slave-girl.

b. What type of literature am I reading?

There are quite a number of different literary *genre* in the Bible:

- historical narrative (Acts)
- dramatic epic (Job)
- poetry (Psalms)
- wise sayings (Proverbs)
- apocalyptic writings (Revelation)
- letter (Paul's 13 New Testament letters)
- Gospel (a collection of Jesus' words and deeds which bear witness to who he was.

We should be asking: Do I take this literally, or figuratively?

c. What do the words mean?

Here we ask questions about how language changes over the years. If you want to know exactly what a word in the

Bible means it can sometimes help to have a first-hand knowledge of Hebrew and Greek, although for most of us having a reliable and accurate translation of the Bible will help 99% of the time.

It is sometimes worth comparing different translations with each other. For example the *King James Version* translation of 1 Thessalonians 5:14 talks about "unruly" people. This word in Greek is *ataktos* and in classical Greek it refers to soldiers who break rank and so cause chaos. But papyri discovered since 1611 indicate that this Greek word stood for a person who skipped work. So when the NIV uses the word "idle" it is a more accurate translation.

d. What if the cultural setting has changed?

This is an important consideration when we attempt to interpret the Bible correctly. There is no doubt that Jesus washed his disciples' feet and said, "I have set you an example that you should do as I have done" John 13:15. So the question is: Why don't we do this to each other? Do we reply and say: We don't have to take any notice of what was done in the first century? Or do we reply and say: We must literally follow this and ignore its cultural setting. There is a third and better way, if we say: Yes we should always follow the principles that Jesus laid down. What is the principle here. As we, in the West, don't walk barefoot along dusty streets, what is the equivalent today? It would be to

gladly perform some kind of humble service for fellow-Christians.

Remember that Scripture interprets Scripture

Or as Dr J. I. Packer has said, "If we would understand the parts, our wisest course is to get to know the whole."

So when interpreting Scripture we look for the general sense of Scripture. We know that God himself is not inconsistent and so we know that Scripture does not contradict itself.

Mary Queen of Scots and John Knox

Mary Queen of Scots once said to John Knox: "Ye interpret the Scriptures in one manner, and they [the pope and his cardinals] in another; whom shall I believe, and who shall judge?"

In reply, John Knox said, "Believe God, who plainly speaks in his Word; And beyond what the Word teaches you, you should neither believe the one nor the other. The Word of God is plain in itself. If there appear any obscurity in one place, the Holy Spirit, who never contradicts himself, explains the same more clearly in other places."

The second coming of Jesus

Jesus' coming will be personal and visible. "This same Jesus, who has been taken from you into heaven, will come back in the same way you have seen him go into heaven" Acts 1:11. Jesus' coming will also be as universal as the lightning. Luke 17:24.

2 THE BIBLE, BOOK BY BOOK: THE OLD TESTAMENT BOOKS OF THE LAW, HISTORICAL AND POETIC BOOKS

THE POETIC BOOKS: JOB THROUGH SONG OF SOLOMON	
JOB	62-63
PSALMS	64-65
PROVERBS	66-67
ECCLESIASTES	68-69
SONG OF SOLOMON	70-71

Introduction

After the book of Genesis, much of the first half of the Old Testament is unfamiliar territory to many Christians. So often we steer clear of it because we just don't know how to start to study it. For example, faced with seemingly endless, meaningless lists of names of people in the first four chapters of 1 Chronicles we may just give up and read another part of the Bible. Chapter 2 of *Bible Study Made Simple* suggests one approach to help us in our study of these historical books of the Old Testament. It suggests a key verse, a key word, a key thought and a key passage for each Bible book. You can read each book in the light of these "keys," asking why they were chosen and in what way they illuminate the biblical text. Once you have a bird's eye view of each Bible book it is much easier to go on and study the whole book.

The book of Genesis

KEYS TO UNLOCK GENESIS	
KEY VERSE	*"In the beginning God created the heavens and the earth"* 6:5.
KEY WORD	*Beginning*
KEY THOUGHT	*God chooses one nation, through whom he will bless all nations.*

Key passages

- Chapters 1–3
- Chapter 15

Names and titles of God

- Elohim [God] 1:1
- Lord God 2:4
- God Most High 14:18
- Sovereign Lord 15:2
- The God who sees 16:13
- God Almighty 17:1
- Judge of all the earth 18:25
- Eternal God 21:33
- The Lord Will Provide 22:14

Genesis' teaching about God

- God is the Creator: 1:1–2:9
- God is holy and judges sin: 3:8-24
- God is merciful: 3:21; 4:15
- God is sovereign over everyone and everything: 18:14; 50:20

Name

The English title for this book is derived from the Greek term meaning "beginnings" or "origins."

The Hebrew title is *bere'shit*, which is taken from Genesis 1:1, "in the beginning."

Author

The book of Genesis does not itself state who it was written by. But both Jewish and Christian traditions claim that Moses wrote the first five books of the Bible. The Old Testament supports Moses writing "the Book of the Law," that is Genesis, Exodus, Leviticus, Numbers and Deuteronomy. "Be careful to obey all the law my servant Moses gave you; do not turn from it to the right or to the left, that you may be successful wherever you go. Do not let this Book of the Law depart from your mouth; meditate on it day and night…" Joshua 1:7, 8.

The New Testament also has many references supporting the Mosaic authorship of the Pentateuch, the five books of the law, as Genesis through Deuteronomy were referred to by the Jews. "I am saying nothing beyond what the prophets and Moses said would happen" Acts 26:22.

Theme and purpose

Genesis answers the big questions of life, such as, Why are were here? and, Where did we come from? Genesis tells us about the beginnings of:

- the world
- humankind
- society
- families
- nations
- sin
- salvation.

Stories

The stories in the book of Genesis are its way of teaching the truth about the above topics. Genesis does not present us with formal teaching but rather a series of stories.

Four key events

There are four main events:

- Creation, 1:1–2:25
- The Fall, 3:1–5:32
- The flood, 6:1–9:29
- The beginning of the nations, 10:1–11:9.

Four key people

There are four main stories about people:

- Abraham, 11:10–25:8
- Isaac, 25:19–26:35
- Jacob, 27:1–36:43
- Joseph, 37:1–50:26.

Genesis in the New Testament

God's plan of redemption is predicted in Genesis.

"And I will put enmity between you and the woman, and between your offspring and hers; he will crush your head, and you will strike his heel" Genesis 3:15. This is the first messianic promise in the Bible.

"Abraham answered, 'God himself will provide the lamb for the burnt offering, my son.'" Genesis 3:21

God's plan of redemption is fulfilled in the New Testament.

"But when the time had fully come,

God sent his Son, born of a woman, born under the law, to redeem those under the law, that we might receive the full rights of sons." Galatians 4:4, 5

"The next day John saw Jesus coming towards him and said, 'Look, the Lamb of God, who takes away the sin of the world!'" John 1:29

OUTLINE		
1.	Creation	1:1–2:24
2.	The Fall of humankind	3:1–5:32
3.	The flood	6:1–9:29
4.	The tower of Babel	10:1–11:9
5.	The story of Abraham	12:1–25:11
6.	The story of Isaac and Ishmael	5:12–27:46
7.	The story of Esau and Jacob	28:1–36:43
8.	The story of Joseph and Jacob's last days	37:1–50:26

The book of Exodus

KEYS TO UNLOCK EXODUS	
KEY VERSE	*"Therefore, say to the Israelites: 'I am the Lord, and I will bring you out from under the yoke of the Egyptians. I will free you from being slaves to them, and I will redeem you with an outstretched arm and with mighty acts of judgment'" 6:6.*
KEY WORD	*Redemption/redeem*
KEY THOUGHT	*God delivers his people from slavery.*

Key passage
Chapters 12–14
As the death of Jesus on the cross is the central event in the New Testament, the Exodus is the central event in the Old Testament, as God delivers his people after the shedding of blood in the Passover.

Names and titles of God

- El-Shaddai – I AM 3:14
- Lord – Jehovah 6:3
- Jehovah-rophe – the Lord who heals 15:26
- Jehovah-nissi – the Lord my Banner 17:8

Who is God like?
The book of Exodus reveals a great deal about the nature of God.

1. God is holy.
2. God provides for his people.
3. God is sovereign.
4. God is concerned for his people.

5. God guides his people.
6. God expects to be worshiped.

Name
The English title for this book is derived from the Greek word *Exodus*, meaning "exit, going out or departure."

The Septuagint, the pre-Christian Greek version of the Old Testament, uses the word *Exodus* as the name of this book. It bases this name after the crucial event described in Exodus 19:1: "After the Israelites *left* Egypt."

The Latin name for this book is *Liber Exodus*, "Book of Departure."

The Hebrew name for this book is *We'elleh Shemoth,* meaning, "And These Are the Names" Exodus 1:1.

Author
See under *Author* "The Book of Genesis."

Theme and purpose
Two great themes are linked together in this book.

First, the theme of redemption is seen in the Passover.

Second, the theme of deliverance is viewed as the Israelites escape from Egypt under the leadership of Moses.

"During the night Phariah summoned Moses and Aaron and said,

- Up! Leave my people, you and the Israelites!
- Go, worship the Lord as you have requested.
- Take your flocks and herds…" Exodus 12:31.

KEY FEATURE IN THE BOOK OF EXODUS: THE TEN COMMANDMENTS EXODUS 20:1-17, *KJV*		
1.	Only one God	And God spake all these words, saying, I am the Lord thy God, which have brought thee out of the land of Egypt, out of the house of bondage. Thou shalt have no other gods before me.
2.	No idols	Thou shalt not make unto thee any graven image, or any likeness of any thing that is in heaven above, or that is in the earth beneath, or that is in the water under the earth. Thou shalt not bow down thyself to them, nor serve them: for I the Lord thy God am a jealous God, visiting the iniquity of the fathers upon the children unto the third and fourth generation of them that hate me; And shewing mercy unto thousands of them that love me, and keep my commandments.
3.	Misuse of God's name	Thou shalt not take the name of the Lord thy God in vain; for the Lord will not hold him guiltless that taketh his name in vain.
4.	The sabbath	Remember the sabbath day, to keep it holy. Six days shalt thou labor, and do all thy work: But the seventh day is the sabbath of the Lord thy God: in it thou shalt not do any work, thou, nor thy son, nor thy daughter, thy manservant, nor thy maidservant, nor thy cattle, nor thy stranger that is within thy gates: For in six days the Lord made heaven and earth, the sea, and all that in them is, and rested the seventh day: wherefore the Lord blessed the sabbath day, and hallowed it.
5.	Honoring parents	Honor thy father and thy mother: that thy days may be long upon the land which the Lord thy God giveth thee.
6.	No killing	Thou shalt not kill.
7.	Marriage	Thou shalt not commit adultery.
8.	No stealing	Thou shalt not steal.
9.	Truth and integrity	Thou shalt not bear false witness against thy neighbor.
10.	Contentment	Thou shalt not covet thy neighbor's house, thou shalt not covet thy neighbor's wife, nor his manservant, nor his maidservant, nor his ox, nor his ass, nor any thing that is thy neighbor's.

OUTLINE		
1.	Deliverance from Egypt	1–15
2.	Journeying to Sinai	16–18
3.	The Law given at Mount Sinai	19–24
4.	Regulations for worship instituted	25–40

The book of Leviticus

KEYS TO UNLOCK LEVITICUS	
KEY VERSE	*"Speak to the entire assembly of Israel and say to them: 'Be holy because I, the Lord your God, am holy'"* 19:2.
KEY WORD	*Holiness*
KEY THOUGHT	*God is holy and the only way to approach him is through sanctification and obedience.*

Key passage
Chapter 16 with its description of the day of atonement.

Name
The English title for this book is derived from the Greek word *Leuitikon* in the Septuagint, which means "that which is about the Levites."

The Hebrew title is *Wayyiqra*, meaning "And he called."

The Talmud called the book of Leviticus both the "Law of the Priests," and the "Law of the Offerings."

Author
See under *Author* in "The Book of Genesis."

Features to note
Leviticus contains the command: "Love your neighbor as yourself" 19:18.

This summary of the Ten Commandments is underlined five times in the New Testament:

- Matthew 19:19
- Mark 12:31
- Luke 10:27
- Romans 13:9
- Galatians 5:14.

God's holiness
In 1 Peter 1:16 Peter quotes from Leviticus 11:44, 45; 19:2; 20:7: "Be holy, because I am holy."

Theme and purpose
Leviticus acted as God's guidebook for his people whom he had just redeemed. It showed how they could worship, serve and obey their holy God.

Learning from numbers

- **56** Leviticus states, 56 times, that God gave laws to Moses.
- **87** The word "holiness" occurs 87 times in Leviticus.
- **65** The word "holy" occurs 65 times in Leviticus.
- **50** 50 times Moses "did as the Lord commanded him." 8:4.
- **300+** The word "sacrifice/s" and the two linked words "offerings" and "oblations" come more than 300 times in Leviticus.
- **49** The word "atonement" comes 49 times.

"The tenth day...is the Day of Atonement.

- Hold a sacred assembly and
- deny yourselves and
- present an offering." Leviticus 23:27

THE OFFERINGS AND SACRIFICES OF THE BOOK OF LEVITICUS			
Its name	*Where found*	*What was used*	*Purpose*
Burnt offering	Leviticus 1	Bullocks, lambs, goats, doves, pigeons. They were wholly consumed on the altar and offered every morning and evening.	It signified dedication
Cereal offering	Leviticus 2	Fine flour, unleavened bread, cakes, wafers and grain: always with salt. A handful was burned on the altar, but the rest was eaten in a holy place by the priests.	This signified thanksgiving.
Peace offering	Leviticus 3	Oxen, goats and sheep. This was a shared sacrifice. The fat was burned, but the rest was eaten by the priests and by the sacrificer and his friends. A meal and drink offering accompanied this sacrifice.	This sacrifice signified fellowship.
Sin offering	Leviticus 4:1–5:13	Bullocks, goats, and lambs. The whole animal was burned outside the camp. A sin offering was made for the whole congregation on all the feast days, especially on the Day of Atonement.	This offering stood for cleansing.
Guilt offering	Leviticus 5:14–6:7	Ram or lamb. The ritual was the same as the sin offering except that the blood was poured and not sprinkled over the surface of the altar. Where wrong had been done to another, restitution was made, including an additional 20%.	This offering represented reconciliation.

OUTLINE	
1. The offerings	1:1–6:7
2. The priesthood	8:1–10:20
3. What is clean and unclean	11:1–15:33
4. The Day of Atonement	16:1-34
5. The meaning of holiness	17:1–22:33
6. Festivals, feasts and other regulations	23:1–27:34

The book of Numbers

KEYS TO UNLOCK NUMBERS	
KEY VERSE	*"...not one of the men who saw my glory and the miraculous signs I performed in Egypt and in the desert but who disobeyed me and tested me ten times–not one of them will ever see the land I promised on oath to their forefathers. No one who has treated me with contempt will ever see it" 14:22, 23.*
KEY PASSAGE	*Chapter 14*
KEY WORD	*Wander*
KEY THOUGHT	*God's people learn that they can only move forwards when they trust him.*

Name of book

The title given to the book comes from its first Hebrew word: *Wayyedabber*, "And he said." But many Jewish writings refer to this book by its fifth Hebrew word, *Bemidbar*, "in the wilderness."

The Greek title in the Septuagint is *Arithmoi*, "Numbers."

The Latin *Vulgate* has *Liber Numeri*, "Book of Numbers."

There are two numberings in this book, in chapters 1 and 26.

"The men twenty years old or more were listed by name" *Numbers 1:18.*

Author

Moses.

Date

c. 1446 to 1406 BC.

Types of Jesus in Numbers

- The Rock: Numbers 20:7-11 with 1 Corinthians 10:4.
- The bronze snake: Numbers 21:6-9 with John 3:14.
- The Star: Numbers 24:17 with Revelation 22:16.
- The Scepter (Ruler): Numbers 24:17 with 1 Timothy 6:14, 15.
- The cities of refuge: Numbers 35 with Hebrews 6:18-20.

Theme

Four of the leading themes in Numbers are:

- God's guidance, 9:15-23
- God's discipline, 1–4
- God's displeasure, 11; 12; 14
- God's provision, 20; 21.

Purpose

God's people spent 40 long years wandering around in the wilderness and learn that they can only make progress as they trust and obey God. In Numbers chapter 14 they rebel against God and so the Lord tells them: "For forty years–one year for each of the forty days you explored the land–you will suffer for your sins and know what it is like to have me against you" 14:34.

Miracles and unusual events in Numbers

1. The cloud by day and the pillar of fire by night: 9:15-23.
2. God's people punished with fire

from God: 11:1-3.

3. God provides quails: 11:4-6, 18-20.

4. A severe plague: 11:31-34.

5. Miriam was punished with leprosy, but healed in answer to prayer: 12:1-15.

6. The earth swallowed up Korah and his rebellious followers: 16:30-35.

7. A plague which killed 14,700 people: 16:41-50.

8. Aaron's staff, budded, blossomed and produced almonds: 17:1-8.

9. Water comes from the rock when struck twice by Moses: 20:7-11.

10. Venomous snakes sent by the Lord as a punishment: 21:5-7.

11. The bronze serpent: 21:8, 9.

12. Balaam's ass which spoke to warn the prophet of his disobedience: 22:21-31.

Learning from numbers

40 God's people wandered for 40 years in the desert on account of their disobedience.

OUTLINE	
1. The camp at Mount Sinai	1–10
2. The journeys in the desert	11–21
3. Preparing to inherit the Promised Land	22-36

The book of Deuteronomy

KEYS TO UNLOCK DEUTERONOMY	
KEY VERSE	*"Love the Lord your God with all your heart and with all your soul and with all your strength"* 6:5.
KEY WORD /PHRASE	*Remember*
KEY THOUGHT	*God requires his people to obey him.*

Key passages

- 6:4-12 • Chapter 8 • Chapter 28

Names and titles of God

- God of gods 10:17
- Lord of lords 10:17
- Rock 32:4, 18, 31
- Most High 32:8
- Eternal God 33:27

Moses as a type of Jesus

Moses fulfills more than anyone else in the Old Testament the following three offices:

- prophet, Deuteronomy 34:10-12
- priest, Exodus 32:31-35
- king, as Moses was a ruler of Israel, Deuteronomy 33:4, 5.

Name

The English title for this book is derived from the Greek words *deuteronomion touto*, which mean "this second law giving."

The Hebrew manuscripts give it the name *'Elleh Haddevarim*, which mean "These are the words," from "These are the words Moses spoke to all Israel" 1:1;
or *Mishmeh Hartorah*, which mean "repetition of the law." This comes from words in Deuteronomy 17:18, "a copy of this law."

Author

Jews and Christians alike have traditionally ascribed the authorship of Deuteronomy to Moses, apart from the few verses which describe his death, 34:5-12. The book of Deuteronomy itself states that Moses wrote it. "So Moses wrote down this law and gave it to the priests, the sons of Levi...After Moses finished writing in a book the words of this law from beginning to end..." Deuteronomy 31:9, 24

Date and setting

c. 1400 BC or 1200 BC. The entire book of Deuteronomy covers only about one month. See Deuteronomy 1:3; 34:8 with Joshua 5:6-12.

The book was written at the end of the 40-year period in the desert and takes place on the plains of Moab, east of the Jordan River and Jericho.

Theme and purpose

Deuteronomy describes how God renewed his covenant with the people of Israel on the Plains of Moab as they prepared to enter the Promised Land. Now that the generation which had received God's covenant at Sinai had died, God sealed his covenant afresh with the people who would capture the land of Canaan.

KEY FEATURE IN THE BOOK OF DEUTERONOMY: THE WORD "REMEMBER"	
The things the book of Deuteronomy says are to be remembered.	
The giving of the law	"Remember the day that you stood before the Lord your God at Horeb, when he said to me, 'Assemble the people before me to hear my words'" 4:10.
God's covenant	"Be careful not to forget the covenant of the Lord your God" 4:23.
Slavery in Egypt	"Remember that you were slaves in Egypt and that the Lord your God brought you out of there with a mighty hand and an outstretched arm" 5:15.
God's judgment	"Remember well what the Lord your God did to Pharaoh and to all Egypt" 7:18.
God's guidance	"Remember how the Lord your God led you all the way in the desert these forty years" 8:2.
God's deliverance	"...so that all the days of your life you may remember the time of your departure from Egypt" 16:3.
God's punishment	"Remember what the Lord your God did to Miriam along the way after you came out of Egypt" 24:9.
God's enemies	"Remember what the Amalekites did to you along the way when you came out of Egypt" 25:17.
Days of old	"Remember the days of old; consider the generations long past" 32:7.

Learning from numbers
50 times God's people are told to "hear" God's teaching. 177 times God's people are told to "keep", "do", "observe" his commands. 21 times God's people are told to have hearts of "love".

Deuteronomy in the New Testament
Jesus quoted the book of Deuteronomy more often than any other Old Testament book. In this sense it was Jesus' favorite Old Testament book.

The New Testament refers to the book of Deuteronomy more than 80 times.

Overview
Look out for three discourses or sermons delivered by Moses:

- 1:1–4:43; 4:44–26:19; 27–43.

OUTLINE		
1.	Covenant history	1:1–3:29
2.	Covenant requirements	4:1–11:32
3.	Covenant laws	12:1–26:19
4.	Covenant renewal	27:1–26
5.	Blessings and curses	28:1-68
6.	Covenant summary	29:1–30:20
7.	The covenant continues	31:1–34:12

The book of Joshua

KEYS TO UNLOCK JOSHUA	
KEY VERSE	*"The Lord gave them rest on every side, just as he had sworn to their forefathers. Not one of their enemies withstood them; the Lord handed all their enemies over to them"* 21:44.
KEY WORD	*Conquered*
KEY PASSAGES	1:1-9; 23:1-16; 24:1-27
KEY THOUGHT	*Israel is to possess the Promised Land.*

Names and titles of God in Joshua

- The living God 3:10
- The Mighty One 22:22

Name of book

The book is named after its leading figure, Joshua.

The Septuagint title is *Iesous Naus*, "Joshua the Son of Nun."

The Latin title is *Liber Josue*, the "Book of Joshua."

Author

The traditional Jewish view is that Joshua wrote this book. Joshua 24:26 is quoted to support this view: "And Joshua recorded these things in the Book of the Law of God." This would not exclude the hand of a later editor putting the book together in the final form in which we now have it. See 4:8, 9; 7:26; 8:28; 24:29, 30.

Date and setting

c. 1350 BC or 1150 BC. The first half of the book describes the conquering of the Promised Land, which took seven years. The second half of the book records how the land was divided up among the 12 tribes of Israel.

Theocratic books

The Old Testament has 12 historical books: Joshua through Esther. The first three historical books, Joshua, Judges and Ruth, are sometimes referred to as the theocratic books, as God rather than any human king, is the center of the life of God's people.

Theme and purpose

Joshua 1:11 sums up the theme of the book: "...take possession of the land the Lord your God is giving you for your own." Joshua gives an historical account of how God's people possessed the Promised Land, in line with God's promise. But the book is more than a history book as the principles God laid down for the military battles are correctly to be applied to spiritual battles Christians face.

Jesus in the book of Joshua

Joshua is a type of Jesus.

Joshua's name means "savior." As Joshua succeeded Moses, so Jesus succeeded the Mosaic Law. See John 1:17; Galatians 3:24, 25; Romans 8:2-4; Hebrews 7:18, 19.

"The commander of the army of the Lord," see 5:13-15, is an appearance of Jesus. Compare with Exodus 3:5.

JOSHUA AND LINKS WITH THE NEW TESTAMENT		
Topic	Ref. in Joshua	Ref. in New Testament
1. God's presence is promised	1:5	Hebrews 13:5
2. Rahab	2:1-6	James 2:25
3. Crossing Jordan with the ark and tabernacle	3:13-17	Acts 7:44, 45
4. The fall of Jericho	6:20	Hebrews 11:30
5. Rahab delivered	6:25	Hebrews 11:31
6. The inheritance given to the Israelites	14:1-2	Acts 13:19
7. Burial of Joseph	24:32	Hebrews 11:22

Achan's secret sin

The town of Ai was not captured at the first attempt. The book of Joshua blames Achan for this.

"Achan replied, 'It is true! I have sinned against the Lord, the God of Israel. This is what I have done: When I saw the plunder a beautiful robe from Babylonia, two hundred shekels of silver and a wedge of gold weighing fifty shekels, I coveted them and took them. They are hidden in the ground inside my tent, with the silver underneath." Joshua 7:20, 21

Overview

The book of Joshua divides itself into three geographic settings:

1. The Jordan River, chapters 1–5
2. Canaan, 6:1–13:7
3. The 12 tribes on both sides of the Jordan, 13:8–24:33.

OUTLINE	
1. Entering the Promised Land	1:1–5:15
2. Conquering the Promised Land	5:13–12:24
3. Dividing up the Promised Land	13:1–22:34
4. Joshua's farewell	23:1–24:33

ACHAN'S SECRET SIN		
Achan's sin is a permanent reminder about what may lay behind failure.		
Topic	Verse/s in Joshua 7	Other references and points to note
Secret sin	1, 21	
God is ignored in the plans	2	In 6:2-5 Joshua relies on God for the strategy to defeat Jericho.
Over-confidence	3	1 Corinthians 10:12
Sin prevents victory	4, 5	
Sin brings shame	5-9	

The book of Judges

KEYS TO UNLOCK JUDGES	
KEY VERSE	*"In those days Israel had no king; everyone did as he saw fit"* 21:25.
KEY WORD	*Delivered*
KEY PASSAGE	*Chapter 2*
KEY THOUGHT	*Corruption from within and oppression from outside result from disobeying God.*

Names and titles of God in Joshua
The Lord is Peace 6:24

Name of book
The Hebrew title is *Shophetim*, which means "judges, rulers or saviors." The equivalent Greek word is used in the Septuagint, *Kritai*. The Latin *Vulgate* used the name *Liber Judicum*, the "Book of Judges."

Author
Unknown. According to tradition Judges was written by Samuel.

Date
Unknown. From the book of Judges itself it is not possible to calculate the exact date of its writing. But it is clear that it was written in the time of the monarchy in the eleventh century BC.

THE JUDGES OF ISRAEL				
The judges of Israel ruled as military leaders, rather than as experts in law.				
	Name	*Notable achievement*	*Years as judge*	*Ref. in Judges*
1.	Othniel	Freed Israel from Mesopotamian oppressors	40	3:7-11
2.	Ehud	Freed Israel from Moabite oppressors	80	3:12-30
3.	Shamgar	Freed Israel from Philistine oppressors	10	3:31
4.	Deborah	Freed Israel from Canaanite oppressors	40	4–5
5.	Gideon	Freed Israel from Midianite oppressors	40	6–8
6.	Tola		23	10:1, 2
7.	Jair		22	10:3-5
8.	Jephthah	Freed Israel from Ammonite oppressors	6	10:6–12:7
9.	Ibzan	[1st of 3 minor judges]	7	12:8-10
10.	Elon	[2nd of 3 minor judges]	10	12:11, 12
11.	Abdon	[3rd of 3 minor judges]	8	12:13-15
12.	Samson	Freed Israel from Philistine oppressors	20	13–16

JOSHUA AND JUDGES COMPARED	
The books of Joshua and Judges throw up many contrasts. A great deal of the book of Judges is given over to details about the failure of the Israelites to trust God, whereas much in the book of Joshua is about the faith and obedience of God's people.	
Joshua	*Judges*
Freedom	Bondage
Progress	Decline
Conquest through belief	Defeat through disbelief
"Then the people answered, 'Far be it from us to forsake the Lord to serve other gods!'" Joshua 24:16.	"The Israelites did evil in the eyes of the Lord; they forgot the Lord their God and served the Baals and the Asherahs" Judges 3:7.
Israel served God, 24:31	Israel was selfish
Israel knew God himself and his power, 24:16-18, 31	Israel did not know God himself or his power, 2:10
In Joshua sin is judged by God	In Judges the people tolerate sin
Enjoyed God's blessings	Experienced grief
Were heavenly-minded	Were earthly-minded

Judges 17:6; 18:1; 21:25 state that the events of this book were written in "days [when] Israel had no king."

Setting
The background to the book of Judges is Israel's failure to drive out all the Canaanites from the Promised Land.

Theme and purpose
The book of Judges has seven cycles in it which follow the same theme under different leaders: foreign oppression, repentance and deliverance.

One sin cycle illustrated: 6:1–8:35
1. The Israelites lived like cave-men before they were prepared to ask God for his help, 6:1-6.

2. A prophet delivers a message of judgment to God's people, 6:7-10.

3. God chooses Gideon because God knows that he is humble and will not take the credit for God's deliverance, 6:11-24.

4. Gideon takes his stand for God and boldly destroys the altar of Baal, even though the people disapproved, 6:25-32.

5. Gideon is not perfect and exposes his own doubts when he puts out two fleeces, 6:33-40.

6. In place of 32,000 men, Gideon takes only 300 men so when the Israelites are defeated everyone knows that God was behind the victory, 7:1-25.

7. The people of Succoth don't help Gideon, who allows gold to replace God, and the people revert to idol worship, 8:1-35.

The book of Ruth

KEYS TO UNLOCK RUTH	
KEY VERSE	*"The women said to Naomi: 'Praise be to the Lord, who this day has not left you without a kinsman-redeemer. May he become famous throughout Israel!'" 4:14.*
KEY WORD	*Kinsman-redeemer*
KEY PASSAGE	*Chapter 4*
KEY THOUGHT	*The story of Ruth displays God's providential care.*

Names and titles of God in Ruth
The Almighty 1:20

Name of book
The Hebrew, Greek and Latin name for this book are all the equivalent of the English word "Ruth."

Author
Unknown.

Date
During the time of the monarchy, in the eleventh century BC.

Setting
The events described in the book of Ruth occurred in the time of Israel's judges.

Theme and purpose
In contrast with the mainly dark period of the judges the book of Ruth illustrates righteousness and faithfulness to God.

It shows how a Gentile woman, Ruth, became great-grandmother to David, and one of Jesus' ancestors.

Boaz, Ruth's husband, was the father of Obed, whose son was Jesse, who was the father of David, Ruth 4:21, 22.

God's sovereignty in the book of Ruth
The books of Ruth depicts God being concerned about the everyday lives of ordinary people. Through his sovereignty human tragedy and despair are transformed.

Four aspects of Ruth
In the short book of Ruth there are four very different types of thing to learn from.

1. A literary consideration
Ruth is both a book of simplicity and great profundity. It is one of the best examples in literature of filial love and piety.

2. An historical consideration
Ruth provides a link between the turmoil of the book of Judges and the new dimension found in the monarchy. Its last word, "David," points forward to the monarchy. In the middle of much unfaithfulness to God found in Judges, Ruth is full of faithfulness, both to family and to God.

"Your people will be my people and your God my God" *Ruth 1:16.*

3. A doctrinal consideration
From the book of Ruth it can be deduced that God's concern reaches beyond the Jews to the Gentiles.

RUTH AND JUDGES COMPARED	
Ruth	*Judges*
Faithfulness, righteousness, purity	Immorality
Ruth was a follower of the true God	Idolatry
Loyalty	Disloyalty
Love	Lust
Peace	War
Kindness	Cruelty
Ruth's obedient faith brought God's blessing	Disobedience leads to sorrow
Spiritual light	Spiritual darkness

RUTH AND ESTHER COMPARED	
Ruth and Esther are the only two biblical books named after women.	
Ruth	*Esther*
A Gentile woman	A Jewish woman
Lived among Jews	Lived among Gentiles
Married a Jewish man in the line of David	Married a Gentile man who ruled an empire
A story about a woman's faith and God's blessing	A story about a woman's faith and God's blessing

4. A moral consideration

Ruth is a model of upright conduct both in her relationship with Noami and in her own marriage.

Four scenes

The book of Ruth can be divided up in different ways. One way is to note the four scenes in the book.

- Scene 1: The country of Moab, 1:1-18.
- Scene 2: A field in Bethlehem, 1:19–2:23.
- Scene 3: A threshing floor in Bethlehem, 3:1-18.
- Scene 4: The city of Bethlehem, 4:1-22.

OUTLINE		
1.	Ruth's loyalty	1
2.	Ruth and Boaz	2
3.	Ruth is redeemed	3:1–4:15
4.	The ancestors of David and Jesus	4:16-22

The books of 1 and 2 Samuel

KEYS TO UNLOCK 1 AND 2 SAMUEL	
KEY VERSE IN 1 SAMUEL	*"But now your kingdom will not endure; the Lord has sought out a man after his own heart and appointed him leader of his people, because you [Saul] have not kept the Lord's command."* 1 Samuel 13:14.
KEY VERSE IN 2 SAMUEL	*"And David knew that the Lord had established him as king over Israel and had exalted his kingdom for the sake of his people Israel"* 2 Samuel 5:12.
KEY WORD IN 1 SAMUEL	*King*
KEY WORD IN 2 SAMUEL	*David*
KEY PASSAGES	*1 Samuel 15; 2 Samuel 5*
KEY THOUGHT IN 1 SAMUEL	*God requires his people to obey him.*

Names and titles of God in 1 and 2 Samuel

- Lord Almighty 1 Samuel 1:3
- Rock 2 Samuel 22:2
- Fortress 2 Samuel 22:2
- Deliverer 2 Samuel 22:2
- Shield 2 Samuel 22:3
- Horn of my salvation 2 Samuel 22:3
- Stronghold 2 Samuel 22:3
- Savior 2 Samuel 22:3
- Support 2 Samuel 22:19
- Lamp 2 Samuel 22:29
- Light of the morning 2 Samuel 23:4
- Brightness after rain 2 Samuel 23:4

Name of book

In the Hebrew Bible 1 and 2 Samuel were a single book. They were known as the "Book of Samuel" or, just, "Samuel."

The Greek Septuagint divided Samuel into two books. It gave the title of *Bibloi Basileion*, "Books of Kingdoms" to them. First Samuel was called *Basileion Alpha*, "First Kingdoms." Second Samuel and First and Second Kings were called "Second, Third, and Fourth Kingdoms."

The Latin *Vulgate* gave the title of *Libri Regum*, "Books of the Kings" to the books of Samuel and Kings.

The Latin Bible went on to combine the Hebrew and Greek titles for First Samuel and called it *Liber I Samuelis*, the "First Book of Samuel."

Author

Unknown. The author of 1 and 2 Samuel is anonymous.

Date

c. tenth century BC.

Setting

1 Samuel describes the transition from the times of the judges of Israel to the establishment of the monarch in Israel.

2 Samuel records the seven years of David's reign over Judah and his 33 years reign over the 12 united tribes of Israel.

Theme and purpose

In I Samuel the rule of the judges ends and the rule of the kings is ushered in.

In 2 Samuel the reign of Israel's second and greatest king, David, is portrayed.

Samuel's life of prayer

Prayer dominated Samuel's life.

1. Samuel was born in answer to the prayers of his mother, Hannah, 1 Samuel 1:10-28.
2. Samuel's name means "asked of God," 1 Samuel 1:20.
3. Samuel's prayer brings about deliverance at Mispah, "this displeased Samuel; so he prayed to the Lord" 1 Samuel 8:6.
4. When Israel asks for their own king so that they can be like the surrounding nations, "This displeased Samuel, so he prayed to the Lord" 1 Samuel 8:6, 21.
5. Samuel never stopped praying for God's people: "And as for me, far be it from me that I should sin against the Lord by failing to pray for you" 1 Samuel 12:23.

The monarchical books

The Old Testament has 12 historical books: Joshua through Esther. 1 and 2 Samuel, 1 and 2 Kings, and, 1 and 2 Chronicles are sometimes referred to as the monarchical books, as they describe the reigns of the kings of Israel.

OUTLINE	
1 Samuel	
1. Eli and Samuel	1–7
2. Samuel and Saul	8–15
3. Saul and David	16–31
2 Samuel	
1. David as a political leader	1–5
2. David as a spiritual leader	6–7
3. David as a military leader	8–10
4. David's sins	11–12
5. Civil war	13–20
6. David's latter years	21–25

The books of 1 and 2 Kings

KEYS TO UNLOCK 1 AND 2 KINGS	
KEY VERSE IN 1 KINGS	*"Yet I will not tear the whole kingdom from him, but will give him one tribe for the sake of David my servant and for the sake of Jerusalem, which I have chosen" 1 Kings 11:13.*
KEY VERSE IN 2 KINGS	*"So the Lord said, 'I will remove Judah also from my presence as I removed Israel, and I will reject Jerusalem, the city I chose, and this temple, about which I said, "There shall my name be"'" 2 Kings 23:27.*
KEY WORDS	*Royalty (1 Kings); Evil (2 Kings)*
KEY PASSAGES	*1 Kings 12; 2 Kings 25*
KEY THOUGHTS	*1 and 2 Kings are a sequel to 1 and 2 Samuel. The theme of 1 Kings is the glory and the division of the kingdom, while the theme of 2 Kings is the history of the divided kingdom.*

Name of book

1 and 2 Kings were originally one in the Hebrew Bible. The Hebrew title for the complete book was *melechim*, "Kings," which was taken from the first word in 1 Kings 1:1.

The Septuagint first divided the book into two books and the Latin *Vulgate* edition followed the Septuagint. The division made in 1 and 2 Kings appears in a most inappropriate place and appears to have been made in an arbitrary place.

Author

Unknown. The talmudic tradition which stated that Jeremiah the prophet wrote 1 and 2 Kings has few supporters today.

Date and setting

Unknown. It was probably written in the sixth century BC by an Israelite prophet in exile in Babylon.

1 KINGS AND 2 KINGS COMPARED	
1 Kings	*2 Kings*
Opens with David, King of Israel	Closes with Nebuchadnezzar, King of Babylon
Solomon's glory	Jehoiachin's shame
The temple is built and consecrated	The temple is violated and destroyed
Begins with blessings for obedience	Ends with judgment for disobedience
Apostasy grows	The consequences of apostasy
The united kingdom is divided	The two kingdoms are destroyed

THE PROPHET ELISHA	
The prophet Elisha is often overshadowed by his illustrious predecessor, Elijah. But there are a number of helpful lessons to learn from Elisha, although he was a very different type of person from Elijah.	
Topic	*Reverence in 2 Kings*
1. Elisha knew how to be God's follower	2:1-8
2. Elisha did not mind doing menial work	3:11
3. Elisha cared about the poor and for the rich	4:1-37
4. Elisha knew when he should keep in the background	5:1-27
5. Elisha demonstrated that he trusted God completely	6:15-17
6. Elisha had great insight into the true nature of people	8:11
7. Elisha was not embarrassed to show his concern, even with tears	8:12
8. Elisha knew about the art of delegation	9:1-4

1 and 2 Kings record the life of Israel over four centuries: from the death of David to the deportation of the people to Babylon.

Theme and purpose

1 Kings records the reign of King Solomon and how after his death the kingdom was sadly divided as the ten northern tribes of Israel set up their own king. Only two tribes made up the southern kingdom of Judah which remained faithful to King David's line. The author is concerned to show how important it was for God's people to keep God's covenant, and how they will be judged by God if they do not.

2 Kings continues the story of the divided kingdom. The 19 kings of Israel were unfaithful to God and Israel is thus taken off into captivity by the Assyrians in 722 BC. Judah came under God's judgment in 586 BC when it was led into exile by the Babylonians.

OUTLINE	
1 Kings	
1. David's last days	1:1–2:11
2. Solomon's golden years	3–10
3. Solomon's decline and death	11
4. Early history of the divided kingdom	12–22
2 Kings	
1. The divided kingdom until Israel falls	1–17
2. The surviving kingdom of Judah	18–25

The books of 1 and 2 Chronicles

KEYS TO UNLOCK 1 AND 2 CHRONICLES	
KEY VERSE IN 1 CHRONICLES	*"Yours, O Lord, is the greatness and the power and the glory and the majesty and the splendor, for everything in heaven and earth is yours. Yours, O Lord, is the kingdom; you are exalted as head over all"* 1 Chronicles 29:11.
KEY VERSE IN 2 CHRONICLES	*"He [Azariah] went out to meet Asa and said to him, 'Listen to me, Asa and all Judah and Benjamin. The Lord is with you when you are with him. If you seek him, he will be found by you, but if you forsake him, he will forsake you'"* 2 Chronicles 15:2.
KEY WORDS	*Covenant (1 and 2 Chronicles)*
KEY PASSAGES	*1 Chronicles 1; 2 Chronicles 7*
KEY THOUGHT	*1 and 2 Chronicles give the spiritual history of Israel.*

Names and titles of God in 1 and 2 Chronicles

- Our father Israel 1 Chronicles 29:10
- Our Leader 2 Chronicles 13:12

Name of book

1 and 2 Chronicles was a single book in the Hebrew Bible. It was then called *Dibere Hayyamin*, meaning, "The words [accounts] of the days," which today might be translated, "The events of the times."

The Septuagint divided the book into two, giving it the name *Paraleipomenon*, "Of things omitted." The "omitted things" referred to the things that have been left out of the books of 1 and 2 Samuel and 1 and 2 Kings.

The English title for 1 and 2 Chronicles comes from the *Vulgate* Bible, *Chronicorum Liber* which refer to the book being "chronicles" of the sacred history of God's people.

Author

Unknown. The text does not identify the author, but according to Jewish tradition Ezra wrote 1 and 2 Chronicles. This view cannot be established for certain. The author of 1 and 2 Chronicles is often referred to as the Chronicler.

Date

1 and 2 Chronicles probably dates from the fifth century BC.

Theme and purpose

The Chronicler gives his view of the history of the kings of Israel. He explains why some had peaceful reigns while others had turbulent reigns. He points to the necessity of being faithful to God. The Chronicler wants his readers to do more than read about the history of God's people. He wants them to learn from their mistakes and their good points. The Chronicler knows that his readers are suffering exile from Jerusalem and may even feel abandoned by God, so he encourages them to believe again in God and his great power.

THEMES FOUND IN 1 AND 2 CHRONICLES COMPARED	
Theme in 1 Chronicles	Theme in 2 Chronicles
Lessons about prayer, 16:8-36; 17:16-27; 29:10-19	Lessons about praise, 5:11-14; 16:14-42; 20:15-30
Lessons about service, 12:23-37; 25:1-8	Lessons about guidance, 18:1-34
Lessons learned from failure, 21:1–22:1	Lessons about suffering, 16:12; 32:24, 25; 33:10-13
Lessons about buildings, 17:3-15; 22:2-19	Lessons about the temple, 2:1–7:22
Lessons about election, 16:13; 28:4-6, 10; 29:1	Lessons about faith, 20:20
Lessons about giving, 29:3-5	Lessons about giving, 24:10; 31:2-21

1 AND 2 SAMUEL AND 1 AND 2 KINGS COMPARED WITH 1 AND 2 CHRONICLES	
1 and 2 Samuel and 1 and 2 Kings	1 and 2 Chronicles
Israel's history from the united kingdom to the two captivities	The focus is on the southern kingdom and the Davidic line
Political history	Religious history
Prophetic authorship	Priestly authorship
Emphasizes the prophetic ministry	Emphasizes the priestly ministry
Emphasizes moral matters	Emphasizes spiritual matters
Emphasizes kings and prophets	Emphasizes the temple and priests
Mostly negative: including rebellion and tragedy	Mostly positive: with hope despite tragedy
A message of judgment	A message of hope
The failings of people	God's faithfulness

OUTLINE			
1 Chronicles		2 Chronicles	
1. Genealogical tables	1–10	1. King Solomon's reign	1–9
2. King David's reign	11–29	2. The reigns of Solomon's successors	10–36

The book of Ezra

KEYS TO UNLOCK EZRA	
KEY VERSE	*"For Ezra had devoted himself to the study and observance of the Law of the Lord, and to teaching its decrees and laws in Israel" 7: 10.*
KEY WORD	*Temple*
KEY PASSAGE	*Chapter 6*
KEY THOUGHT	*Ezra teaches how God's people can be restored to himself.*

Name of book

The English word "Ezra" is derived from the Aramaic form of the Hebrew word *ezer*. Because 1 and 2 Chronicles and Ezra and Nehemiah were thought of as one continuous history Ezra and Nehemiah were originally bound as one book.

In the Latin Bible Ezra is called *Liber Primus Esdrae*, "First book of Ezra," while Nehemiah is called "Second Ezra."

Author

While the book of Ezra certainly contains some of Ezra's diaries or memoirs it does not state who the author of the book is. However Ezra seems to be the best candidate for the author to some scholars, but other scholars feel that Ezra probably did not write this book.

Date and setting

The exact date of writing of Ezra is unknown, but it was probably in the fifth century BC.

Carrying on the history of God's people from 2 Chronicles, Ezra shows how God fulfilled his promise of his people's return to Jerusalem after 70 years exile. The first return was led by Zerubbabel and, decades later, the second return was led by Ezra himself.

The restoration books

The Old Testament has 12 historical books: Joshua through Esther. The books of Ezra, Nehemiah and Esther are sometimes referred to as the restoration books, as they describe the return of a remnant of the Jews to their homeland after their 70-year captivity.

EZRA AND THE NEW TESTAMENT		
While there are no direct quotations from Ezra in the New Testament there are a number of themes in Ezra which are also covered in the New Testament.		
Topic	*In Ezra*	*In New Testament*
Doing what pleases God	1:5	Philippians 2:13
Events working out for good	8:22	Romans 8:28
The enormity of sin	9:6	Revelation 18:5
Greater judgment if sin continues	9:14	John 5:14
Guilt before God	9:15	Romans 3:19

Theme and purpose

The Jews deported from Jerusalem were taken to Babylon by the Babylonians. But in 539 BC Babylon was captured by Persia and three years later Cyrus decreed that the Jews should be allowed to return to Palestine. Around 50,000 Jews returned to Jerusalem under Zerubbabel and nearly 2,000 returned with Ezra in 458 BC.

Woven into Ezra's historical account are his teaching about God, worship and the seriousness of sin.

Lessons to learn about God from Ezra

- God keeps his promises, 1:1
- God achieves his own ends, 1:5
- God is always totally holy, 4:3; 9:15
- God transforms unpromising and evil situations, 5:3–6:12
- God is involved in people's lives, 7:27, 28
- God answers prayer, 8:23, 31
- God is totally good, 3:11

Special features to note

The book of Ezra contains 7 letters or official documents.

1. One Hebrew document

The decree of Cyrus: 1:2-4

2. Six Aramaic documents

- a. Rehum's accusation against the Jews: 4:11-16
- b. Artaxerxes' reply to Rehum: 4:17-22
- c. Tattenai's report: 5:7-17
- d. Cyrus' decree: 6:2-5
- e. Darius' reply to Tattenai: 6:6-12
- f. Artaxerxes' authorization to Ezra: 7:12-26

OUTLINE	
1. Cyrus' decree	1
2. List of returning exiles	2
3. Rebuilding of the temple	3–6
4. Second return under Ezra and his reforms	7–10

The book of Nehemiah

KEYS TO UNLOCK NEHEMIAH	
KEY VERSE	*"So the wall was completed on the twenty-fifth of Elul, in fifty-two days" 6:15.*
KEY WORD	*Walls*
KEY PASSAGE	*Chapter 1*
KEY THOUGHT	*God requires his people to obey him.*

Names and titles of God in Nehemiah

"The king said to me, 'What is it you want?'

Then I prayed to the God of heavens."
The God of heaven 2:4

Name of book

See *"Name of book"* in *The book of Ezra.*

Author

From the opening words in Nehemiah 1:1, "The words of Nehemiah son of Hacaliah" many have concluded that Nehemiah is the author of the whole book, as some portions of it, 1:1–7:5; 12:27-43; 13:4-31 are indeed "the words of Nehemiah." However the matter is complicated because some scholars think that Nehemiah 7:6–12:26 was written by Ezra, and because Nehemiah 7:5-73 is nearly the same as Ezra 2:1-70. Some scholars therefore side with the ancient Jewish tradition that 1 and 2 Chronicles, as well as Ezra and Nehemiah were all written by Ezra.

Date and setting

Fifth century BC.

Theme and purpose

In the book of Ezra the temple was rebuilt, but the walls of Jerusalem still lay in ruins. Nehemiah obtained permission, the necessary supplies and money from the king of Persia and set about rebuilding Jerusalem's walls.

When did Nehemiah pray?

1. When he heard about the state of Jerusalem, 1:4-11
2. When he asked King Artaxerxes if he could return to Jerusalem, 2:4
3. When he faced opposition, 4:4, 9
4. When false accusations were leveled at him, 6:8, 9
5. When the work was finished, 13:14

Nehemiah's work

Nehemiah is the best example in the Old Testament of somebody who combined work and prayer.

1. He worked out what had to be done in Jerusalem before he started, 2:11-16.
2. He organized everybody to work so that they knew what to do, 3:1-32.
3. He inspired others to work by his own example, 2:17-18; 4:6, 23.
4. He believed that the work he had to do had been given him by God, 6:3.

OUTLINE		
1.	Reconstruction of the walls	1–7
2.	Reformation of the people	8–13

The book of Esther

KEYS TO UNLOCK ESTHER	
KEY VERSE	*"For if you remain silent at this time, relief and deliverance for the Jews will arise from another place, but you and your father's family will perish. And who knows but that you have come to royal position for such a time as this?" 4:14*
KEY WORD	*Deliverance*
KEY PASSAGE	*Chapter 6*
KEY THOUGHT	*God is in ultimate control of the world.*

Author

Unknown. The book does not state the name of its author although it is clear that it was most probably written by someone who was fully conversant with Jewish feasts and who lived in Persia's capital, Susa, where the story is set.

Date and setting

The book was probably written by a Jew in Susa during Xerxes' reign, 486–465 BC.

Theme and purpose

This book explains the origin of the Feast of Purim which Jews celebrate between 13th and 15th Adar (February – March). Esther 9:20-32; 3:7.

The book illustrates how the Jews are God's special people who are protected by him.

The book of Esther also shows how God controls events, even when everything seems hopeless.

Special features to note

This book never mentions God but his providential overruling of events is obvious to those who read it with the eye of faith.

OUTLINE		
1.	Esther replaces Vashti as queen	1:1–2:23
2.	Haman's plot against Mordecai	3
3.	Haman's plot is discovered	4–7
4.	The king reverses his decree	8
5.	The Jews celebrate	9–10

The book of Job

KEYS TO UNLOCK JOB	
KEY VERSE	*"But he knows the way that I take; when he has tested me, I shall come forth as gold" 23:10.*
KEY WORD	*Tested*
KEY PASSAGES	*Chapters 28; 42*
KEY THOUGHT	*God's "answer" to Job in his suffering is to reveal to him a glimpse of his infinite wisdom and greatness.*

Name of God the Holy Spirit in Job
The breath of the Almighty 32:8

Name of book
The Hebrew name for this book is *Iyyob*, has been translated as "persecuted" but also as "to come back" or "repent." The Greek and Latin titles for this book are Iob.

Author
The book of Job does not give us the name of its author and it is not possible from reading the book to say who wrote it.

Date and setting
There are a wide variety of opinions about the date of the book of Job. Some believe that it is the oldest book in the Bible while some place it as late as the exile.

Some scholars point out that the date of Job himself and his historical setting may be many centuries before the writing of the book of Job. It has been argued from a verse like 19:24, with its reference to inscribing with an iron tool, that the book was set in or after the twelfth century BC, as iron was not in common use in the ancient Near East before then. Possible date: *c.* 1400 BC or 1200 BC.

Theme and purpose
Job was a righteous man who was struck down will serious illness and suffering. He has three sets of debates with three

of his friends, who all argue that his suffering has been brought about because of his sin. While the book of Job does not provide any simplistic answer to the problem of personal suffering Job discovers, in the last chapter of the book, God's majesty and power and worships him and submits to him.

Teaching found in the book of Job
1. Teaching about God's character and his deeds
In Job God is pictured as being sovereign and even the devil cannot act without his permission. That God is the Creator and Sustainer of the world is acknowledged by Job and his friends. 5:8-16; 9:2-13; 11:7-9; 12:10, 13-25; 25:2-6; 26:5-14; 34:10-15; 35:10, 11; 36:22-33; 37:1-24; 38:1–39:30; 40:8–41:34.

2. Teaching about the weakness of humankind
Job himself illustrates how weak and sinful humans are. The book also shows the brevity of our lives. Only in a life beyond this one can wrongs be righted. 4:17-21; 5:7; 7:1-10; 9:2, 25, 26; 14:1, 2, 4, 7-12; 15:14-16; 25:4-6.

Poetry books
All the Bible books up to the book of Job (Genesis through Esther) are historical in character and except for a few isolated instances of poetry are written in prose. The next five books,

Job through the Song of Solomon are often referred to as the poetry books as they are in Hebrew meter.

The New Testament and Job
Job is only mentioned once in the New Testament: James 5:11. However, the many profound questions and longings raised in the book of Job are answered in the New Testament.

1. Humankind's longing for someone to arbitrate between us and God. Compare Job 9:33 with 1 Timothy 2:5.
2. Is there any life after death? Compare Job 14:14 with John 11:25.
3. God is my advocate. Compare Job 16:19 with Hebrews 9:24.
4. My Redeemer lives. Compare Job 19:25 with Hebrews 7:25.
5 Where can God be found? Compare Job 23:3 with John 14:6.

OUTLINE	
1. Satan tests Job and Job's friends arrive	1–3
2. The first round of discussions	4–14
3. The second round of discussions	15–21
4. The third round of discussions	22–31
5. Elihu joins in	32–37
6. God speaks	38:1–42:6
7. Job is rewarded	42:7-17

The book of Psalms

KEYS TO UNLOCK PSALMS	
KEY VERSE	*"Ascribe to the Lord the glory due to his name; worship the Lord in the splendor of his holiness" 29:2.*
KEY WORD	*Worship*
KEY PASSAGES	*1; 22; 23; 24; 37; 100; 119; 121; 150*
KEY THOUGHT	*The theme of the book of Psalms is "My God and me," or "Our God and us."*

Names and titles of God in the Psalms

- Shield 3:3
- One who bestows glory 3:3
- One who lifts up my head 3:3
- My rock 18:2
- My fortress 18:2
- My deliverer 18:2
- My God 18:2
- The horn of my salvation 18:2
- My stronghold 18:2
- My shepherd 23:1
- King of glory 24:8
- My light 27:1
- My rock of refuge 31:2
- Strong fortress 31:2
- The God of truth 31:5
- My help 54:4
- Lord God Almighty 59:5
- God of Israel 59:5
- The rock that is higher than I 61:2
- Holy One of Israel 71:22
- God of Jacob 75:9
- God Most High 78:35
- Shepherd of Israel 80:1
- My Father 89:26
- My refuge 91:2
- The great God 95:3
- Holy and awesome 111:9
- The Lord 118:27
- Watches over you 121:5
- Your shade 121:5
- God of gods 136:2
- Lord of lords 136:3
- Sovereign Lord 140:7
- My loving God 144:2

Name of book

The Hebrew name for this book was *Sepher Tehillim*, "Book of praises." The Greek word *Psalmoi* used by the Septuagint means poems sung to the accompaniment of musical instruments. The Latin title was *Liber Psalmorum*, "Book of Psalms."

Author

There are numerous authors of the psalms. David is credited with 73 of them: 3–9; 11–32; 34–41; 51–65; 68–70; 86; 101; 103; 108–110; 122; 124; 131; 133; and 138–145. There are 50 anonymous psalms, two of which, numbers 2 and 95, the New Testament tells us were by David. The other named authors are Asaph, the sons of Korah, Solomon, Moses the man of God, Heman and Ethan.

Date and setting

The psalms were Israel's hymnbook and are a collection of prayers and praises. They come from a long period of Israel's history, stretching back at least as far as the time of David and perhaps stretching forward to after Israel's exile in Babylon. Date: *c.* 1400 BC or 1200 BC.

Theme and purpose

Many of the psalms were used first of all for personal worship of God, but many were also written for public worship, especially for worship in the temple on festival days. The psalms express Israel's worship of God over the centuries.

Jesus in the Psalms

A number of the psalms anticipated Jesus' life and ministry. Centuries after the psalms were written Jesus came as Israel's promised Messiah, the anointed one.

The psalms, in common with the Gospels, emphasize different facets of who Jesus was and what work he would do.

Jesus Christ, the king

Portrayed in Matthew's Gospel.

- Psalm 2: Christ is rejected as King by the nations.
- Psalm 18: Christ is Protector and Deliverer.
- See also: Psalms 20; 21; 24; 47; 110; 132.

Jesus Christ, the servant

Portrayed in Mark's Gospel.

- Psalm 17: Christ is Intercessor.
- Psalm 22: Christ is the dying Savior.
- See also: Psalms 23; 41; 69; 109.

Jesus Christ, the Son of Man

Portrayed in Luke's Gospel.

- Psalm 8: Christ is made a little lower than the angels.
- Psalm 16: Christ's resurrection is promised.
- Psalm 40: Christ's resurrection is realized.

Jesus Christ, the Son of God

Portrayed in John's Gospel.

- Psalm 19: Christ is Creator.
- Psalm 102: Christ is eternal.
- Psalm 118: Christ is the chief Cornerstone.

Overview

The Psalms are "a collection of collections" and made up of five books.

- Book one: 1–41
- Book two: 42–72
- Book three: 73–89
- Book four: 90–106
- Book five: 107–150

The book of Proverbs

KEYS TO UNLOCK PROVERBS	
KEY VERSE	*"The fear of the Lord is the beginning of knowledge, but fools despise wisdom and discipline"* 1:7.
KEY WORD	*Wisdom*
KEY PASSAGES	*Chapters 8; 31*
KEY THOUGHT	*The book of wisdom brings together the collective wisdom of Israel.*

Name of book

The Hebrew title to this book, *Mishle Shelomoh*, and the Greek title, *Paroimiai Salomontos*, both mean "Proverbs of Solomon" as Solomon wrote so many of the proverbs. In the Latin title, *Liber Proverbiorum*, "Book of Proverbs," the words *pro* "for", and, *verba* "words," are combined to indicate how proverbs concentrate many words into a few.

Author

Solomon, who wrote 3,000 proverbs according to 1 Kings 4:32, is credited with writing most of the book of Proverbs. Others mentioned as contributors are "the wise" Proverbs 22:17; 24:23; Agur son of Jakeh and King Lemuel.

Date

Solomon's proverbs date back to the tenth century BC.

Theme and purpose

The book of Proverbs is one of the few Bible books to state its purpose:

"...for attaining wisdom and discipline;
for understanding words of insight;
for acquiring a disciplined and
prudent life, doing what is right
and just and fair;
for giving prudence to the simple,
knowledge and discretion to the
young–
let the wise listen and add to their
learning, and let the discerning
get guidance–
for understanding proverbs and
parables, the sayings and riddles
of the wise." *Proverbs 1:2-6*

Wisdom in the letter of James and the book of Proverbs

1. The tongue

Ref. in Proverbs	Ref. in letter of James
a. 12:18-19	1:26
b. 15:1-2	3:5
c. 18:21; 21:6	3:6
d. 21:23	1:19; 3:8
e. 25:23	4:1

2. Human and divine wisdom found in James resembles wisdom found in Proverbs. Human wisdom in James 3:15, 16 is:
   a. earthly 14:2
   b. natural 7:18
   c. demonic 27:20
   d. jealous 6:34
   e. selfish 28:25
   f. disorderly 11:29
   g. evil 8:13

PROVERBS IN THE NEW TESTAMENT

There are at least 14 quotations and allusions to the Proverbs in the New Testament. In addition to that there are also numerous ideas which are common to them both.

Topic	Reference in Proverbs	Reference in New Testament
Punishment	3:1-12	Hebrews 12:5, 6; Revelation 3:19
Grace to the humble	3:34	James 4:6; 1 Peter 5:5
Love your enemies	25:21, 22	Romans 12:19, 20
Evil feet	1:16	Romans 3:15
Self-esteem	3:7	Romans 12:16
Love covering sin	10:12	1 Peter 4:8
Evangelism	11:30	1 Corinthians 9:19; James 5:20
Good for evil	17:13; 20:22	Romans 12:17; 1 Peter 3:9
Sparing words	17:27	James 1:19
Power of the tongue	18:21	Matthew 12:37
Help for the poor	19:17	Matthew 25:42-46
The reality of sin	20:9	1 John 1:8
No respect for parents	20:20	Matthew 15:4
Training children	22:6	Ephesians 6:4; 2 Timothy 3:15
Humility	25:6, 7	Luke 14:8-10
Uncertain future	27:1	James 4:13-15
Knowing truth	28:5	John 7:17; 1 Corinthians 2:15

God's wisdom in James 3:17 is:
    a. pure 15:26
    b. peaceable 3:1, 2
    c. gentle 11:2
    d. reasonable 14:15
    e. full of mercy 11:17
    f. constant 21:6
    g. without hypocrisy 28:13

OUTLINE

1. Why the way of wisdom is the superior way   1–9

2. Solomon's main collection of proverbs   10:1–22:16

3. Proverbs not written by Solomon   22–31

The book of Ecclesiastes

KEYS TO UNLOCK ECCLESIASTES	
KEY VERSE	*"Now all has been heard; here is the conclusion of the matter: Fear God and keep his commandments, for this is the whole duty of man"* 12:13.
KEY WORD	*Meaninglessness (Vanity AV)*
KEY PASSAGES	*Chapters 8; 12*
KEY THOUGHT	*Life without God is meaningless.*

Name of book
The Hebrew title for this book is *Qoheleth*. It is a word that is rarely found and in the Bible it is only found in this book, 1:1, 2, 12; 7:27; 12:8-10. It has been translated in a wide variety of ways: preacher, teacher, debater and even leader of an assembly. It literally means "one who convenes an assembly," and so has come to be translated as "one who addresses an assembly, a preacher."

The Greek Bible gives this book the title *Ekklesiastes*, which is taken from the word *ekklesia* meaning assembly, church or congregation. The Latin Bible uses the title *Ecclesiastes* meaning someone who speaks in front of an assembly.

Author
According to the Jewish talmudic tradition there is no doubt that Solomon wrote this book. From the opening verse, "The words of the Teacher, son of David, king of Jerusalem," 1:1, the authorship of this book is settled for many. For Solomon was David's son and

was also king of Jerusalem. While Solomon is not mentioned by name as the author there are many passages which indicate that he was indeed the author: 1:1, 12, 16; 2:4-9; 7:26-29; 12:2.

However some scholars point out some features in the book that might point to someone other than Solomon: that the word "son" in 1:1 can refer to a much later descendant; and that in 2:9 the writer appears to speak of predecessors in Jerusalem before him when there had only been one – King David.

Date and setting
If Solomon wrote this book that would place it in the middle of the tenth century BC.

Scholars who do not think Solomon wrote the book have placed its writing as early as the third century.

Theme and purpose
The Teacher or Preacher of Ecclesiastes shows how running after wealth, worldly wisdom, power or pleasure lead nowhere, are unsatisfying and leave one feeling that life is meaningless. If this book is not viewed as a tract written with a worldly person in mind one might reach the false conclusion that it is written by a fatalist. But the writer points out that the only ultimate fulfillment in life is God himself. So his conclusion is, "Fear God and keep his commandments" 12:13.

Life under the Sun, Life under the Son

1:3 What advantage is work under the sun?

The one who started a good work in you will carry it on to completion, see Philippians 1:6.

1:9 There is nothing new under the sun

In Christ everyone is a new creation, see 2 Corinthians 5:17.

1:14 All deeds are vanity under the sun

No labor is in vain when it is done in the Lord, see 1 Corinthians 15:58.

6:12 Under the sun everyone is mortal

Believing in Jesus results in everlasting life, see John 3:16.

9:3 Everyone dies under the sun

Life in Jesus is eternal life, see 1 John 5:11.

OUTLINE	
1. Illustrations of vanity	1:1-11
2. Life appears to be meaningless but is a gift from God	1:12–11:6
3. In old age and death remember that God is Judge	11:7–12:7
4. Obey God	12:8-14

Song of Solomon

KEYS TO UNLOCK SONG OF SOLOMON	
KEY VERSE	*"Many waters cannot quench love; rivers cannot wash it away. If one were to give all the wealth of his house for love, it would be utterly scorned"* Songs of Solomon 8:7.
KEY WORD	*Love*
KEY PASSAGE	*Chapter 1*
KEY THOUGHT	*The beauty of human love is God's gift.*

Name of book

The Hebrew title, *Shir Hashirim*, "The song of songs," is taken from the opening verse, "Solomon's Song of Songs" 1:1. As Solomon's name is also in this verse the book is also known by the title, "Song of Solomon." The Greek title, *Asma Asmaton* and the Latin title, *Canticum Canticles* also mean "The Song of Songs," in the sense of "The best song."

Author

The opening verse, "Solomon's Song of Songs," and the seven references to Solomon, 1:1, 5; 3:7, 9, 11; 8:11, 12 and other verses about the "king," 1:4, 12; 7:5, are all taken to support the traditional view that King Solomon wrote this book.

Scholars who do not think that Solomon was the author point out that "Solomon's Song of Songs" could just mean that here is a song for or about Solomon.

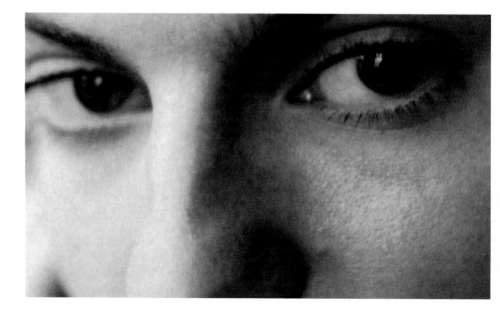

Date and setting
Assuming that Solomon was the author the Song of Solomon would have been written in the middle of the tenth century BC.

Interpretation of the book
There are two main views about how this book should be interpreted. The allegorical view states that this book shows God's love for his people. God is illustrating his love for his bride Israel and Christ is showing his love for his church. There are other Old Testament passages where the husband/wife relationship is viewed in a symbolic way: Ezekiel 16; 23; Hosea 1–3. While this may be a valid application of the Song of Solomon there is nothing in the actual book to indicate that this is the correct interpretation, and there are no New Testament references to the Song of Solomon.

The second view says that the book should be read at face value, always remembering that love is a gift from God. 8:6, 7 has been taken to support this view as it is an example of the way that wisdom literature, as in Proverbs 1–9 and Job 18 where wisdom is personified, describes the tenderness of an amorous relationship. For this reason the Song of Solomon has been described as a collection of love poems or reflections.

A picture of the Christian church
If the Song of Solomon is taken to be a picture of the Church, then the bride-groom stands for Jesus, and the bride for the Christian believer. This theme often occurs in other parts of the Bible.

The Bridegroom
1. His love covers all the defects of the bride, 4:7; 7:10.
2. He rejoices over her, Isaiah 62:5.
3. He gave his life for her, Ephesians 5:25.
4. He will come to claim her for his own, 1 Thessalonians 4:16, 17.
5. He will present her to his Father as a glorious bride, Ephesians 5:27.

The bride
1. Feels her unworthiness, 1:5.
2. Loves the Bridegroom because he first loved her, 2:16; 1 John 4:19.
3. Is purified and dressed in a robe of righteousness, Revelation 19:8.
4. Wears the jewels of divine grace, Isaiah 61:10.
5. Looks for the Bridegroom's appearing, Hebrews 9:28.
6. Invites others to the wedding, Revelation 22:17.

OUTLINE	
1. The first meeting	1:1–2:7
2. The second meeting	2:8–3:5
3. The third meeting	3:6–5:1
4. The fourth meeting	5:2–6:3
5. The fifth meeting	6:4–8:4
6. The beauty of love	8:5-14

3 THE BIBLE, BOOK BY BOOK: THE OLD TESTAMENT PROPHETIC BOOKS

CONTENTS

Introduction

Major and minor prophets

The prophetical books of the Old
Testament take up about one quarter of
the Bible. These 17 books have been
classified as "major" and "minor"
prophets. The "major" prophets are not
more important than the "minor" ones,
but just greater in length, except for
Lamentations. The five "major"
prophetic books are: Isaiah, Jeremiah,
Lamentations, Ezekiel and Daniel.

The 12 so-called "minor" prophets of
the Old Testament ("minor" only in
terms of length, not in terms of
importance), Hosea through Malachi are
probably the least known part of the
whole Bible. Chapter 3, by setting out
the name, author, date, setting, theme
and purpose of these books, gives a
straightforward way of becoming
acquainted with these books.

Work out a couple of things about
each of these prophecies: were they
given before or after the exile? Were they
directed to the northern kingdom of
Israel, or to the southern kingdom of
Judah? If you like you can make your
own lists. You'll discover that only three
of the 12 books, Haggai, Zechariah and
Malachi, are addressed to the Israelites
after they have returned from their
enforced exile. And you'll see that only
three of the 12 books, Jonah, Amos and
Hosea, are addressed to the northern
kingdom of Israel. Once you have your
bearings it is much easier to go on to
further study.

The book of Isaiah

KEYS TO UNLOCK ISAIAH	
KEY VERSE	*"But he was pierced for our transgressions, he was crushed for our iniquities; the punishment that brought us peace was upon him"* Isaiah 53:5.
KEY WORD	*Salvation*
KEY PASSAGES	*Chapter 53*
KEY THOUGHT	*God will judge evil but offers mercy and forgiveness to all who will respond with faith towards him.*

Names and titles of God in Isaiah

- The Holy One of Israel 1:4
- The Lord Almighty 6:3
- The Rock eternal 26:4
- God of all the earth 54:5
- Your Maker 54:5
- Your Redeemer 54:5
- The Mighty One of Jacob 60:16
- Our Father 64:8
- The Potter 64:8

Name of book
The book is called "Isaiah" in the Jewish, Greek and Latin Bibles, meaning "Yahweh is salvation."

Author and date
The traditional Jewish and Christian view of the authorship of this book is that one man, the eighth-century prophet Isaiah, wrote every chapter of it.

Setting
Isaiah's lengthy ministry extended over 50 years. It started in about 740 BC and ended in about 680 BC. "The vision concerning Judah and Jerusalem that Isaiah son of Amoz saw during the reigns of Uzziah, Jotham, Ahaz and Hezekiah, kings of Judah" Isaiah 1:1. Isaiah lived in Jerusalem when the city was under military threat. Israel was in the final stages of collapse. Assyria captured the ten tribes of the northern kingdom of Israel in 722 BC, 2 Kings 17. Isaiah gave an unpopular message: "Do not trust in any alliances with other countries, trust only in God's power." While the two southern tribes of Judah were heading for judgment as well due to the corruption of her society, political life and religious life, she would not be wiped out. In his mercy God promised that one day, from Judah, a Savior for the whole world would arise. He is Isaiah's "Servant of the Lord," and Isaiah has four extended poems or psalms about him: 42:1-7; 49:1-7; 50:4-11; 52:13–53:12.

Theme and purpose
Isaiah recounts the sin of Israel and pronounces God's judgment on his people. Isaiah says that the surrounding nations will also be judged by God, but that this will be followed by God's blessing. After chapters about King Hezekiah Isaiah concludes by consoling Israel with a message of future salvation and restoration.

Learning from numbers
28 The word "salvation" comes 28 times in Isaiah. **21** Isaiah is mentioned by name 21 times in the New Testament.

Isaiah in the New Testament
Isaiah is the most-quoted prophet in the New Testament. His name occurs 21 times in the New Testament and it is quoted more often that all the other prophetic books put together. There are at least 85 quotations or allusions to the book of Isaiah in the New Testament.

Isaiah, "the Shakespeare" of the prophets, has also been called the "evangelical prophet" because of his numerous and clear messianic prophecies. Isaiah chapter 53 is alluded to many times in the New Testament.

Salvation in Isaiah
1. Wells of salvation: to satisfy us. "Surely God is my salvation; I will trust and not be afraid. The Lord, the Lord, is my strength and my song; he has become my salvation. With joy you will draw water from the wells of salvation" 12:2, 3.
2. Joy of salvation: to keep us praising God. "Let us rejoice and be glad in his salvation" 25:9.
3. Walls of salvation: to protect us. "We have a strong city; God makes salvation its wall and ramparts" 26:1.
4. Everlasting salvation: to keep us forever, 45:17.

5. Day of salvation: our present possession, 49:8.
6. Arm of salvation: to lift us up when we fall, 59:16.
7. Helmet of salvation: to endure as a soldier on active duty, 59:17.
8. Garments of salvation: to enable us to stand unashamed before God, 61:10.
9. Light of salvation: to guide us, 62:1.

OUTLINE	
1. Judah will be judged	1:1–5:30
2. The call of Isaiah	6:1-13
3. Isaiah and King Ahaz	7–12
4. Judgments on foreign nations	13–27
5. Jerusalem under Assyrian domination	28–35
6. Isaiah and King Hezekiah	36–39
7. The return of the exiles	40–66

The book of Jeremiah

KEYS TO UNLOCK JEREMIAH	
KEY VERSE	*"I have loved you with an everlasting love; I have drawn you up again and you will be rebuilt, O Virgin Israel" Jeremiah 31:3.*
KEY WORD	*Return*
KEY PASSAGES	*Chapters 2; 31*
KEY THOUGHT	*God requires more than admission or regret of sin: he demands repentance.*

Names and titles of God in Jeremiah
The Lord Our Righteousness 23:6

Name of book
In the Hebrew Bible, the Greek Bible and the Latin Bible the title of this book is "Jeremiah."

Author
The opening verse of this book states that Jeremiah was its author: "The words of Jeremiah son of Hilkiah, one of the priests at Anathoth in the territory of Benjamin" 1:1.

Date and setting
Jeremiah's prophecies stretched over more than a 40-year period from the thirteenth year of King Josiah, 627 BC, until the destruction of Jerusalem and the start of the exile in 587/6 BC.

Theme and purpose
Judah was in a state of moral decline and Jeremiah was called by God to an unpopular prophetic ministry of proclaiming God's judgment on the unrepentant nation. Jeremiah, despite being persecuted, pronounced that Judah would fall but that God would establish a new covenant with his people.

Special features to note
Unlike Ezekiel's prophecy in the book of Ezekiel, Jeremiah's prophecies are not in chronological order in the book of Jeremiah. The following reading plan gives an approximate chronological order of the book.

1:1–7:15; 26; 7:16–20:18; 25; 46–51; 36:1-8; 45; 36:9-32; 35; 21–24; 27–31; 34:1-7; 37:1-10; 34:8-22; 37:11–38:13; 39:15–18; 32–33; 38:14–39:14; 52:1-30; 40–44; 52:31-34.

Learning from numbers
- **164** Babylon, who will carry out God's judgment on Judah is mentioned 164 times in Jeremiah.
- **47** The word return comes 47 times in Jeremiah.
- **13** Backsliding is mentioned 13 times in Jeremiah.

OUTLINE		
1.	Jeremiah's call	1:1-19
2.	Warnings to Judah	2–35
3.	Jeremiah's suffering	36–38
4.	Jerusalem falls	39–45
5.	Judgment on other nations	46–51
6.	The people exiled	52

The book of Lamentations

KEYS TO UNLOCK LAMENTATIONS	
KEY VERSE	*"Because of the Lord's great love we are not consumed, for his compassions never fail"* 3:22.
KEY WORD	*Tears*
KEY PASSAGE	*Chapter 3*
KEY THOUGH	*In a times of complete devastation remember God's faithfulness and mercy.*

Names and titles of God in Lamentations

- God of gods 10:17
- Lord of lords 10:17
- Rock 32:4, 18, 31
- Most High 32:8
- Eternal God 33:27

Name of book
The Hebrew title for this book, *Ekah*, "And how," is taken from the opening words of the book. The Greek title is *Threnoi*, meaning "dirges" or "laments," and the Latin title *Threni* means "tears" or "lamentations." The Septuagint has this introduction to Lamenatations: "And it came to pass after Israel was led into captivity that Jeremiah sat weeping and lamenting and lamented this lamentation over Jerusalem." The sub-title in the *Vulgate* is *Id est lamentations Jeremiae prophetae*, "The Lamentations of Jeremiah."

Author
According to Jewish and Christian tradition, Jeremiah wrote this book, although the book itself is anonymous. Nobody was better placed to write these laments over the destruction of God's city than an eyewitness of the devastating event who had also spent the last 40 years of his life warning Judah that it would take place.

Date and setting
Sixth century BC, most probably within ten years of the destruction of Jerusalem in 586 BC.

Theme and purpose
Lamentations are Judah's funeral song over the fallen city of Jerusalem.
  "How deserted lies the city…" Lamentations 1:1. Jeremiah's deep sadness over this calamity is apparent in the vivid descriptions of the defeat and destruction of the city.
  From the Middle Ages Jews have read this book on the eve of every Sabbath at the Wailing Wall in Jerusalem, as they commemorate the destruction of their city. But this book is not without hope, which is found in God's mercy when divine pardon is sought.

OUTLINE	
1. Jerusalem's devastation	1
2. God's anger with his people	2
3. Judah's hope in God's mercy	3
4. Judah's future	4
5. Judah asks for forgiveness	5

The book of Ezekiel

KEYS TO UNLOCK EZEKIEL	
KEY VERSE	*"I will give you a new heart and put a new spirit in you; I will remove from you your heart of stone and give you a heart of flesh" 36:26.*
KEY WORD	*Restore*
KEY PASSAGES	*Chapters 36; 37*
KEY THOUGHT	*God's glory has departed from his temple but it will return.*

Names and titles of God in Ezekiel
The Lord is there 48:35

Name of book
In the Hebrew Bible, the Greek Bible and the Latin Bible the title of this book is "Ezekiel." The name appears twice in this book, but nowhere else in the Old Testament.

Author
Ezekiel explains that the book bearing his name is a record of his life and prophecies from 597 to 570 BC. According to the opening verse of the book he was with the exiles by the river Kebar when he was given a vision of God.

Date and setting
Sixth century BC. The king of Babylon, Nebuchadnezzar, deported to Babylon King Jehoiachin with ten thousand of the leading citizens of Israel. Much to the anger of these exiles, Ezekiel prophesied in Ezekiel 1–24 that

Jerusalem would fall, as a result of God's judgment. In 587 BC, as a result of a rebellion by the puppet government left in Jerusalem, Nebuchadnezzar did totally destroy Jerusalem and took a larger group of people into exile. Ezekiel 25–32 are prophecies of judgment on the surrounding nations. Ezekiel 33–39 were prophecies made after the fall of Jerusalem in which Ezekiel encourages God's people to repent and to become a new community serving God. The final chapters, 40–48, look forward beyond the return of the exiles to the end times and to a vision of the new Jerusalem.

Special features to note
Ezekiel used more prophetic symbolism, as he personally acted out his prophecies, than any other Old Testament prophet.
"Therefore, son of man,

- pack you belongings for exile…
- dig through the wall and
- take your belongings out through it" Ezekiel 12:3, 5.

OUTLINE		
1.	Ezekiel's call	1–3
2.	Prophecies against Jerusalem	4–24
3.	Prophecies against the surrounding nations	25–32
4.	Prophecies about the future	33–39
5.	Prophecies about the new Jerusalem	40–48

The book of Daniel

KEYS TO UNLOCK DANIEL	
KEY VERSE	*"In my vision at night I looked, and there before me was one like a son of man, coming with the clouds of heaven. He approached the Ancient of Days and was led into his presence"* 7:13.
KEY WORD	*Kingdom*
KEY PASSAGES	*Chapters 2; 9*
KEY THOUGHT	*The prophetic book of Daniel is primarily concerned with the end times.*

Names and titles of God in Daniel

- God of heaven 2:44
- God of gods 2:47
- Lord of kings 2:47
- Revealer of mysteries 2:47
- Most High God 3:26
- King of heaven 4:37
- The living God 6:20
- The Lord God 9:3
- The great and awesome God 9:4

Name of book

The Hebrew, Greek and Latin name for

this book are all the equivalent of the English word "Daniel," meaning "God is my judge."

Author

Daniel is named as the author of this book in 9:2; 10:2 and 12:4.

Date and setting

Sixth century BC. Daniel was a prisoner of war in Babylon, one of the exiles whom King Nebuchadnezzar had deported from Jerusalem.

Theme and purpose

In their exile the Jews were demoralized and felt as if they had been abandoned by God. Psalm 137:1 sums up how they felt. "By the rivers of Babylon we sat and wept when we remembered Zion." They were so fed up they could not sing: "How can we sing the songs of the Lord while in a foreign land?" *Psalm 137:4* Daniel answered this question by saying through his book that God is still God, even in Babylon.

Learning from numbers

57 The word "kingdom" is found 57 times in Daniel.

OUTLINE		
1.	Daniel in Babylon	1
2.	Visions in Babylon	2–6
3.	Visions of world empires	7–12

The book of Hosea

KEYS TO UNLOCK HOSEA	
KEY VERSE	*"I will heal their wayward-ness and love them freely, for my anger has turned away from them" 14:4.*
KEY WORD	*Return*
KEY PASSAGES	*Chapters 3; 14*
KEY THOUGHT	*God continues to love his people, despite their faithlessness.*

Name of book

The Hebrew, Greek and Latin name for this book are all the equivalent of the English word "Hosea," which means "salvation." "Joshua" and "Jesus" come from the same Hebrew root word as the Hebrew word for "Hosea."

Author

Hosea. Hosea was the only writing prophet to come from the northern kingdom of Israel, to whom his prophecies were directed. Nothing is known about Hosea outside his book.

Date

The middle of the eighth century BC.

Setting

Hosea prophesied for about 40 years in most turbulent times, during the dying decades of Israel. During this time four of the kings of Israel, Zechariah, Shallum, Pekahiah and Pekah, were all murdered by their successors. Israel is often referred to as "Ephraim," as in 5:3, after the largest tribe in Israel.

Theme and purpose

Hosea was married to Gomer. Gomer's unfaithfulness to Hosea was a picture of Israel's unfaithfulness to God, just as Hosea's care for Gomer, even when she became a prostitute, was a picture of God's love for Israel, despite their unfaithfulness to him. Hosea exposes Israel's sins and shows them up in contrast to God's holiness. But, because of God's faithfulness, Hosea teaches that Israel will be restored in the future, after it has suffered God's judgment.

Learning from numbers

15 "Return" comes 15 times in Hosea.

OUTLINE	
1. Hosea's family	1–3
2. God will judge Israel	4–13
3. The promise of restoration	14

The book of Joel

KEYS TO UNLOCK JOEL	
KEY VERSE	*"And afterwards, I will pour out my Spirit on all people. Your sons and daughters will prophesy, your old men will dream dreams, your young men will see visions" 2:28.*
KEY WORD	*The day of the Lord*
KEY PASSAGE	*Chapter 2*
KEY THOUGHT	*The only hope for God's people is for them to repent before God's judgment arrives.*

Name of book

The Hebrew name *Jo'el* means "Yahweh is God." *Joel* is an apt title for this book with its emphasis on God's sovereign work in history. The Greek name for this book is *Ioel* and the Latin is *Joel*.

Author

Joel is named as the author of this prophecy, 1:1.

"The word of the Lord that came to Joel son of Pethuel."

Joel has been called the prophet of the Pentateuch as there are over 20 references to the first five books of the Old Testament in his prophecy. Joel has also been called:

- the prophet of "the rent heart"
- the prophet of revival
- the prophet of Pentecost.

Date

This book is traditionally dated in the ninth century BC.

Setting

A calamity had just hit the southern kingdom of Judah. A recent plague of locusts had decimated the land. Joel uses this to illustrate the coming day of the Lord which will be a terrible day of judgment.

Theme and purpose

In view of God's impending judgment Joel urges the people of Judah to repent.

OUTLINE		
1.	The plague of locusts	1:1-20
2.	The coming day of the Lord	2:1-32
3.	The nations are judged	3:1-21

The book of Amos

KEYS TO UNLOCK AMOS	
KEY VERSE	*"This is what he showed me: The Lord was standing by a wall that had been built true to plumb, with a plumb-line in his hand" 7:8.*
KEY WORD	*Plumbline, a symbol of judgment*
KEY PASSAGE	*Chapter 9*
KEY THOUGHT	*God's punishment on Israel is certain.*

Names and titles of God in Amos

- The Lord God Almighty 4:13
- The Lord 5:8

Name of book

The name *Amos*, comes from the Hebrew word *amas*, which means, "to lift a burden," and, so, "to carry." So Amos' name meant "Burden" or "Burden-bearer." He bore the burden of declaring God's judgment on rebellious Israel.

Author

Amos, a keeper of sheep and a farmer who looked after groves of sycamore-figs, 7:14. While he came from Tekoa, 1:1, a town six miles south of Bethlehem, Amos delivered his eight prophetic denouncements to the people in the northern kingdom of Israel.

Date

The opening verse of Amos' prophecy places the book in the time of two kings: one king of Israel, Jeroboam, 782–753; and one king of Judah, Uzziah,

767–739. This places Amos' prophecies in the middle of the eighth century BC.

Setting

Business was booming in Israel. But Amos points out that injustice and greed lurk below the surface. True worship of God had been usurped by the worship of idols.

Theme and purpose

Because of the nation's indifference towards God, like a rotting basket of fruit, it was ripe for God's judgment.

Amos and the rest of the Old Testament
Amos and the Pentateuch

a. Compare Amos 2:7 with Deuteronomy 23:17, 18.
b. Compare Amos 2:8 with Exodus 22:26.
c. Compare Amos 2:12 with Numbers 6:1-22.
d. Compare Amos 4:4 with Deuteronomy 14:28; 26:12.
e. Compare Amos 4:5 with Leviticus 2:11; 7:13.

OUTLINE		
1.	Eight prophecies	1:1–2:16
2.	Three sermons	3:1–6:14
3.	Five visions	7:1–9:10
4.	Five promises	9:11-15

The book of Obadiah

KEYS TO UNLOCK OBADIAH	
KEY VERSE	*"The day of the Lord is near for all nations. As you have done, it will be done for you; your needs will return upon your own head" verse 15.*
KEY WORD	*Edom*
KEY PASSAGE	*This book has 21 verses in its only chapter*
KEY THOUGHT	*The Edomites, who were always against God's people, would be judged by God.*

Name of book
"Obadiah" means "worshiper of Yahweh." The book is named after the prophet Obadiah.

Author
The author of the books is given as "Obadiah." There are 13 Obadiahs in the Old Testament. Nothing is known about Obadiah himself and he was probably an obscure prophet.

Date
The sixth century BC.

Setting
If verses 11-14 are correctly linked to the Babylonian attacks on Jerusalem, (605–586) this would make Obadiah a contemporary of Jeremiah.

Theme and purpose
This prophecy is concerned with the relationship between Judah and Edom, its southern neighbor. Obadiah prophesies against Edom, predicting its fall, because it always opposed Judah.

Edom refused to allow Judah to pass through its land on their way to the Promised Land. The Edomites opposed Saul but were subdued by David and Solomon. But the Edomites fought against Jehoshaphat and rebelled against Jehoram. The Edomites applauded the destruction of Jerusalem in 586 BC, as the psalmist notes, "Remember, O Lord, what the Edomites did on the day Jerusalem fell. 'Tear it down,' they cried, 'tear it down to its foundations'" Psalm 137:7.

Obadiah's prophecies about Edom being destined to fall came true in 312 BC. Edom remained a heap of ruins forever.

Learning from numbers
21 Obadiah, with its single chapter made up of 21 verses, is the shortest book in the Old Testament.

Overview
The constant struggle between Esau and Jacob continued in the form of the continuing struggle between their descendants in the nations of Edom and Israel.

OUTLINE	
1. Prophecy against Edom	verses 1-14
2. The day of the Lord and Judah's blessing	verses 15-21

The book of Jonah

KEYS TO UNLOCK JONAH	
KEY VERSE	*"But I, with a song of thanksgiving, will sacrifice to you. What I have vowed I will make good. Salvation comes from the Lord"* 2:9.
KEY WORD	*Preach*
KEY PASSAGE	*Chapter 3*
KEY THOUGHT	*Chapter 3 describes a large revival as the wicked city of Nineveh cries out to God, believes in him, and proclaims a fast.*

Names and titles of God in jonah

The God of heaven 1:9

Name of book

The Hebrew word for *Yonah* means a "dove." The book is named after its main character, Jonah.

Author

The opening verse of the book introduces the reader to Jonah, who is identified as being the "son of Amittai."

Jonah's mission is clearly stated:

"Go to the great city of Nineveh and preach against it, because its wickedness has come up before me" Jonah 1:2.

While the book itself is anonymous, tradition ascribes it to Jonah. This Jonah was a prophet in the reign of Jeroboam II of Israel according to 2 Kings 14:25, and came from Gath Hepher in Zebulun, Joshua 19:10, 13.

Date

Probably in the eighth century BC, before the fall of Samaria in 722-721.

Setting

Jonah was a contemporary of King Jeroboam II of Israel (782–753 BC). This makes Jonah a near contemporary of Elisha the prophet and also of Amos and Hosea. Jonah's mission meant that he had to go to one of Israel's most dreaded enemies, Assyria, and to the capital, Nineveh, of a nation whose cruelty was legendary.

Theme and purpose

The purpose of the book of Jonah is plainly stated in 4:11: "Should I not be concerned about that great city?" Jonah had grown up to think that God specially favored his own nation and that one should rejoice over the calamities of ungodly nations and even wish for God's wrath to descend on them.

This book is a rebuke to such a view as it portrays God's gracious forgiveness to a Gentile town.

OUTLINE		
1.	Jonah refuses to obey God	1:1-17
2.	Jonah's repentance and prayer	2:1–3:10
3.	Jonah's remorse as Nineveh turns to God	4:1-10
4.	God's concern for Nineveh	4:11

The book of Micah

KEYS TO UNLOCK MICAH	
KEY VERSE	*"He has showed you, O man, what is good. And what does the Lord require of you? To act justly and to love mercy and to walk humbly with your God" 6:8.*
KEY WORD	*Hear*
KEY PASSAGE	*Chapter 7*
KEY THOUGHT	*Micah's messages alternate between God's judgment on Judah and God's restoration of Judah.*

Name of book
The name of the book is taken from the prophet Micah, whose name means, "Who is like God?"

Author
Micah.

Date
According to Micah 1:1 these prophecies took place during the reigns of three kings of Judah: Jotham (750–732), Ahaz (735–715) and Hezekiah (715–686). In Micah 1:6 the fall of Samaria, 722–721, is prophesied.

Setting
Micah directed most of prophecies to the northern kingdom of Israel, but some towards the southern kingdom of Judah. Micah was a contemporary of Hosea in the northern kingdom, and of Jeremiah in the court of Jerusalem.

Theme and purpose
Micah's prophecies reflect the social conditions of Israel before Hezekiah introduced his religious reforms.

- False prophets preached in order to become wealthy.
- The leaders of Israel indulged in violence.
- The priests were motived by greed.
- The landlords crushed the poor.
- Judges were open to bribes.
- Businessmen used inaccurate scales.

Overview
Micah's prophecies concentrate on the link between genuine spirituality and being honest. Micah predicts that Zion's glory will be much greater in the future when the Messiah, who will be born in Bethlehem, 5:2, will come to deliver them. "Out of you will come me one who will be ruler over Israel."

OUTLINE		
1.	Judgment is predicted	1:1–3:12
2.	Restoration is predicted	4:1–5:15
3.	A call to repentance	6:1–7:20

The book of Nahum

The book of Habakkuk

KEYS TO UNLOCK NAHUM	
KEY VERSE	"The Lord is good, a refuge in times of trouble. He cares for those who trust him" 1:7.
KEY WORD	Jealous
KEY PASSAGE	Chapter 3
KEY THOUGHT	Nahum prophesies about the impending judgment on the Ninevites.

KEYS TO UNLOCK HABAKKUK	
KEY VERSE	"…but the righteous will live by his faith" 2:4.
KEY WORD	Faith
KEY PASSAGE	Chapter 3
KEY THOUGHT	God's holiness will be seen as his judgment falls on Judah by the hand of the Babylonians.

Name of book

The book is named after the prophet, whose name means "comfort, consolation" and is a shortened form of Nehemiah, meaning "comfort of Yahweh."

Author

The opening verse of this prophecy states that the book is about Nahum's vision. Nahum is from Elkosh but nothing else is known about him.

Date and setting

Seventh century BC. Probably between 663 and 612. The fall of the city of Nineveh, which occurred in 612, is the focus of this book.

OUTLINE	
1. The destruction of Nineveh is predicted	Chapter 1
2. The destruction of Nineveh is described	Chapter 2
3. The reason for the destruction of Nineveh is given	Chapter 3

Name of book

The book takes its name from the prophet Habakkuk, 1:1.

Author

Apart from being a contemporary of Jeremiah little is known about Habakkuk, 1:1; 3:1.

Date

Seventh century BC.

Theme and purpose

Habakkuk starts by casting his prophecy in the form of an argument with God about his seemingly unjust way, but then moves on to respond with his great declaration of faith in God. He concluded by stating: "The Sovereign Lord is my strength" 3:19.

OUTLINE	
1. The problems of Habakkuk	1:1–2:20
2. The praise of Habakkuk	3:1-19

The book of Zephaniah

The book of Haggai

KEYS TO UNLOCK ZEPHANIAH	
KEY VERSE	"Seek the Lord, all you humble of the land, you who do what he commands. Seek righteousness, seek humility; perhaps you will be sheltered on the day of the Lord's anger" 2:3.
KEY WORD	Seek
KEY PASSAGE	Chapter 3
KEY THOUGHT	God's judgment on Judah and the nations.

KEYS TO UNLOCK HAGGAI	
KEY VERSE	"'Go up into the mountains and bring down timber and build the house, so that I may take pleasure in it and be honored,' says the Lord" 1:8.
KEY WORD	Build
KEY PASSAGE	Chapter 2
KEY THOUGHT	Haggai encouraged the returned exiles to rebuild the temple in Jerusalem.

Name of book
Zephaniah's name means "Yahweh hides," or, "Yahweh has hidden."

Author
Zephaniah was the great great-grandson of Hezekiah, King of Judah.

Date
From Zephaniah 1:1 this prophecy must have been given during King Josiah's reign, 640–609, which makes Zephaniah a contemporary of Jeremiah and Nahum.

Theme and purpose
Zephaniah states that the coming day of the Lord will be in the form of judgment on the nations.

OUTLINE	
1. Judgment in the day of the Lord	1:1–3:8
2. Salvation in the day of the Lord	3:9-20

Name of book
The book is named after the prophet Haggai, whose name means "festal" which has led to speculation that Haggai was born during one of the three pilgrimage feasts (Unleavened Bread, Pentecost or Weeks, and Tabernacles).

Author
Haggai's name comes nine times in this book and he is also mentioned in Ezra 5:1 and 6:14 where he works with the prophet Zechariah encouraging the temple's rebuilding.

Date
520 BC. See Haggai 1:1 and Zechariah 1:1.

OUTLINE	
1. Rebuild the temple	1:1-15
2. The glory of the temple	2:1-9
3. The blessings of obedience	2:10-19
4. The promise to Zerubbabel	2:20-23

The book of Zechariah

KEYS TO UNLOCK ZECHARIAH	
KEY VERSE	*"Rejoice greatly, O Daughter of Zion! Shout, Daughter of Jerusalem! See, your king comes to you, righteous and having salvation, gentle and riding on a donkey, on a colt, the foal of a donkey"* 9:9.
KEY WORD	*Return*
KEY PASSAGE	*Chapter 14*
KEY THOUGHT	*God is in absolute control of life and history.*

Name of book
The book is named after the prophet Zechariah, whose name means "God remembers," or, "God has remembered."

Author
Zechariah was a prophet, but also a priest, 1:1, as were Jeremiah and Ezekiel. He was born in Babylonia and went to Jerusalem with Zerubbabel, the governor, and Joshua, the high priest. He was a younger contemporary of Haggai.

Date
Zechariah's prophecies started in 520 and continued to at least 480 BC.

Setting
Zechariah's prophecies come from the post-exilic period and are set against the background of the Jewish restoration from their exile in Babylonia.

Theme and purpose
The main purpose of the first eight chapters of Zechariah's book is to encourage, rebuke and motivate God's people to complete the restoration of the temple.

Chapters 9–14 focus on God's faithfulness towards Israel through the work of the Messiah. There are numerous references in Zechariah to the coming Messiah:

- to his humble coming, 6:12
- to his humanity, 13:7
- to his rejection and betrayal for 30 pieces of silver, 13:7
- to his priesthood, 6:13
- to his kingship, 9:9
- to his coming in glory, 14:4
- to his building the Lord's temple, 6:12, 13
- to his reign, 9:10
- to him establishing a time of peace and prosperity, 9:9, 10.

Overview
Zechariah employs visions, symbols, images and statements to emphasize that so long as we do God's will we need live in fear of nothing.

OUTLINE		
1.	Introduction	1:1-6
2.	Eight visions	1:7–6:15
3.	Four messages	7:1–8:23
4.	Two burdens	9:1–14:21

The book of Malachi

KEYS TO UNLOCK MALACHI	
KEY VERSE	*"But for you who revere my name, the sun of righteousness will rise with healing in its wings. And you will go out and leap like calves released from the stall"* 4:2.
KEY WORD	*The day of the Lord*
KEY PASSAGE	*Chapter 3*
KEY THOUGHT	*Malachi signals the close of Old Testament prophecy and ushers in 400 years of silence.*

Name of book
The book of Malachi is named after the prophet Malachi whose name means "My messenger."

Author
The book is ascribed to Malachi, 1:1, but no other information is given about this prophet.

Date
The middle of the fifth century BC. Malachi's book is the last prophecy on the Old Testament era.

Setting
Malachi prophesied against the same events that Nehemiah had to deal with:

- corrupt priests, 1:5–2:9, see also Nehemiah 13:1-9;
- the neglect of tithes and offerings, 3:7-12, see also Nehemiah 13:10-13;
- intermarriage with pagan wives, 2:10-16, see also Nehemiah 13:23-28.

Theme and purpose
In the first part of the book the sins of Israel are the focus of attention. Malachi sketches out a courtroom scene in which Israel is asking God the following questions:

- How have you loved us? 1:2
- How have we despised your name? 1:6
- In what ways have we broken the covenant you gave to our fathers? 2:10
- How have we wearied God? 2:17

In the second part of the book Malachi reassures God's people that a time is coming when the wicked will be judged and those who fear God will be blessed.

This time will be preceded by a messenger, who is identified in the New Testament as being John the Baptist, who will prepare the way of the Lord.

Overview
Malachi exposes the general religious decline among God's people who had returned to Jerusalem from exile.

OUTLINE	
1. Israel's sins are listed	1:1–2:17
2. God promised judgments and blessings will come	3:1–4:6

4 THE BIBLE, BOOK BY BOOK: THE NEW TESTAMENT, MATTHEW THRU' ACTS

Introduction

The authorship of the Gospels has become a much debated field of biblical research. For many people the traditional authors, Matthew, Mark, Luke and John, are the writers of the four Gospels, even though, strictly speaking, each Gospel is anonymous. The only way to find out their authorship is to study the internal and the external evidence in each Gospel.

In the case of Matthew this is of little help because nowhere does the Gospel itself say that Matthew was its author. If Matthew 9:10ff has no bearing on this discussion, there are not even any direct hints in this Gospel concerning its authorship.

Matthew became thought of as the author of the first Gospel on account of a saying of Papias, who, in AD 130, wrote: "Matthew compiled the oracles (*to logia*) in Hebrew and everyone translates them as best he could." This lack of evidence for the authorship of the first Gospel from within the Gospel itself distresses some, but "more important that individual authorship is the truth of the gospel to which all four evangelists bear witness" (F. F. Bruce).

As we study this, and other issues in the Gospels, the words of a former Archbishop of Canterbury are worth bearing in mind: "Our reading of the gospel story can be and should be an act of personal communion with the living Lord" (William Temple).

The Gospel of Matthew

KEYS TO UNLOCK MATTHEW	
KEY VERSE	*"Then Jesus came to them and said, 'All authority in heaven and on earth has been given to me'"* 28:18.
KEY WORD	*King*
KEY PHRASE	*This took place to fulfil what the Lord had said*
KEY PASSAGE	*Chapter 16, Peter's confession about Christ*
KEY THOUGHT	*By carefully selecting dozens of Old Testament quotations Matthew documents Jesus' claim to be Messiah.*

Names and titles of God in Matthew

- Lord 2:15
- Lord your God 4:7
- Father 5:16
- Our Father 6:9
- Heavenly Father 6:26
- Lord of heaven and earth 11:25
- The living God 16:16
- God of Abraham, Isaac and Jacob 22:32
- God of the living 22:32

Name of book

The book derives its name from a man named Matthew. Matthew means "Gift of the Lord." In Mark 2:14 and Luke 5:27 he is also called "Levi." At an early date this Gospel was entitled *Kata Matthaion*, "According to Matthew."

The word "Gospel" was a later addition.

Author

In the early church the church fathers were unanimous in believing that Matthew, one of Jesus' 12 apostles, was the author of this Gospel.

In recent years some scholars have cast doubt on this as they maintain that much of Matthew's Gospel relies on the writing of Mark's Gospel. Their argument is that if Matthew himself was an eyewitness of the events in his Gospel he would not need to rely on Mark's Gospel at all. However, even if it is agreed that some of Matthew's Gospel relies on Mark's Gospel, it is quite possible that Matthew did this deliberately to endorse the united apostolic witness to Jesus.

Date

It is not possible to give one certain date, but this Gospel was probably written between AD 58 and 70.

Setting

It is not possible to say whether this Gospel was written in Palestine or in Syrian Antioch. The Jewish nature of the Gospel has led many to opt for Palestine.

Theme and purpose

Matthew's Gospel was written for Jews, by a Jew, about a Jew. By using many references to Jesus fulfilling specific promises made in the Old Testament Matthew is making sure that the reader realizes that the long-awaited Messiah has come in the person of Jesus Christ.

Special features of Matthew's Gospel

1. It is the fullest Gospel.
2. It is a very orderly Gospel. It alternates between sections of Jesus' teaching and sections which describe Jesus' actions.
3. Matthew speaks about the kingdom of heaven which is especially appropriate to Jews, whereas the other Gospels speak about the kingdom of God.
4. Of the four Gospel writers only Matthew speaks about the church and how it should be run.

Learning from numbers

32 Matthew uses 32 different names to refer to Jesus in his Gospel. **33** The phrase the "kingdom of heaven" comes 33 times in Matthew's Gospel. **43** The word "Father" is used 43 times in Matthew's Gospel.

The Readers

While it is true that Matthew's Gospel would have special appeal to Jewish readers, Gentiles (non-Jews) are by no means ignored:

- the Gentile women found in Matthew's genealogy of Jesus;
- the Gentiles, wise men, who worshiped Jesus;
- the field being the world in the parable of the weeds, 13:38;
- the great commission in which Jesus said, "make disciples of all nations" 28:19.

Overview

Matthew's Gospel has been used as a teaching manual ever since it was written. It is ideal for this as it sets out Christian teaching in such a systematic way. It presents:

- the claims of Jesus
- the credentials of Jesus
- the authority of Jesus
- the ethical teaching of Jesus
- the theological teaching of Jesus.

OUTLINE	
1. Jesus' early life	1:1–4:25
2. The Sermon on the Mount	5:1–7:29
3. Jesus' ministry (1)	8:1–12:50
4. Jesus' parables	13:1-52
5. Jesus' ministry (2)	13:53–19:30
6. Jesus in Jerusalem	20:1–25:46
7. Jesus' trial, death, resurrection and commission	26:1–28:20

The Gospel of Mark

KEYS TO UNLOCK MARK	
KEY VERSE	*"For even the Son of Man did not come to be served, but to serve, and to give his life as a ransom for many"* 10:45.
KEY WORD	*Serve*
KEY PHRASE	*At once*
KEY PASSAGE	*Chapter 8, Peter's confession about Jesus*
KEY THOUGHT	*This is clearly stated in Mark's opening verse: "The beginning of the gospel about Jesus Christ, the Son of God." Mark's Gospel is all about the person and mission of Jesus Christ.*

Names and titles of God in Mark

- Father 8:38
- The God of Abraham, Isaac, and Jacob 12:26
- God of the living 12:27
- Lord 12:29
- Abba, Father 14:36

Name of book
The ancient title for this Gospel was *Kata Markon,* "According to Mark."

Author
There is no one verse in Mark's Gospel which proves that this Gospel was written by Mark, who was called by his Hebrew name of "John" in Jewish circles, and hence is sometimes referred to as "John Mark," see Acts 12:12, 25; 15:37.

The evidence about Mark writing the Gospel which bears his name goes back

to Papias (c. 140) who said:

- Mark was closely linked with Peter, from whom he learned all about Jesus' life;
- this information about Jesus Mark gleaned from Peter's sermons;
- Mark's Gospel is faithful to all Mark learned about Jesus from Peter.

From this it is believed that Mark's Gospel is made up of Peter's sermons which were carefully presented and shaped by Mark.

Who was John Mark?
Mark, the author of Mark's Gospel, is also the John Mark found in the New Testament.

1. John Mark was the cousin of Barnabas, Colossians 4:10.
2. John Mark lived in Jerusalem with his mother, Mary, Acts 12:12, and the church met in his home.
3. He accompanied Paul and Barnabas on a missionary journey, Acts 13:5.
4. In Cyprus Mark left Paul and Barnabas and returned to Jerusalem, where he would have had plenty of opportunity of talking with Peter.
5. As Peter refers to Mark as, "my son Mark," 1 Peter 5:13 it has been concluded that Peter may have helped Mark to belief in Jesus.
6. The young man mentioned in Mark 14:51, 52 has been identified as being Mark, but there is insufficient evidence to be certain about this.

Date

Nobody knows for sure when Mark wrote his Gospel. But because of the prophecy about the destruction of the temple, 13:2, it seems reasonable to conclude that it was written before AD 70. It was probably written between AD 55 and AD 65.

Setting

Early church tradition from the writings of Irenaeus and Clement of Alexandria state that Mark wrote his Gospel from Rome, where Peter was martyred. 2 Timothy 4:11 and 1 Peter 5:13 confirm that Mark was linked with Peter and in Rome at about the time of Peter's martyrdom.

One factor in Mark's mind as he wrote his Gospel may well have been the impending persecution of the Christians in Rome which took place in AD 64-67, following the fire in Rome of AD 64. Mark has many explicit and cloaked references to discipleship and suffering, 1:12, 13; 3:22, 30; 8:34-38; 10:30, 33, 34; 13:8, 11-13.

Theme and purpose

Mark emphasizes the cross of Jesus as being a divine necessity, 8:31; 9:31; 10:33, and pinpoints its human cause, 12:12; 14:1, 2; 15:10. Throughout his Gospel Mark lays great stress on Jesus being the Son of God, 1:1, 11; 3:11; 5:7; 9:7; 12:1-11; 13:32; 15:39, while also stressing his humanity, 3:5; 6:6, 31, 34; 7:34; 8:12, 33; 10:14; 11:12.

Special features of Mark's Gospel

1. Mark is the shortest Gospel.
2. Mark is the simplest Gospel.
3. Most scholars believe that Mark was the first Gospel to be written.
4. Mark and his mystery: Mark presents Jesus-with-a-secret to his readers, as he often shows that Jesus discouraged publicity about himself:
   a. Demons were told to keep quiet, 1:25, 34.
   b. Those Jesus healed were told not to talk about their healing, 1:44.
   c. Jesus' own followers were told not to tell other people that he was the Messiah, 8:30.
   d. Jesus told his followers about "the secret of the kingdom of God," 4:10-12.

Jesus knew that people had a political and human deliverer in mind when they thought of the Messiah and did not want his ministry to be confused with this.

OUTLINE	
1. Introduction and Jesus' early ministry	1:1–9:1
2. Transfiguration and visit to Jerusalem	9:2–10:52
3. Jesus final week	11:1–15:47
4. Jesus' resurrection	16:1-8 (20)

The Gospel of Luke

KEYS TO UNLOCK LUKE	
KEY VERSE	*"For the Son of Man came to seek and to save what was lost"* 19:10.
KEY WORD	*Save*
KEY PHRASE	*Son of Man*
KEY PASSAGE	*Chapter 15, with its three parables of the Lost Sheep, the Lost Coin and the Lost Son, illustrating the heart of the gospel*
KEY THOUGHT	*In his Gospel, Luke presents Jesus Christ as the Perfect Man who came to seek and to save sinful humanity.*

Names and titles of God in Luke

- Lord 1:6
- The Most High 1:35
- Lord God 1:68
- Father 2:49
- The Most High God 8:28
- Lord of heaven and earth 10:21

Name of book

Kata Loukon, "According to Luke," was attached to this Gospel at a very early date.

Author

Luke's name is nowhere to be found in his Gospel, but there is compelling evidence that he wrote the Gospel that bears his name.

Acts is the companion volume to Luke's Gospel, and both are addressed to the same person, Theophilus, Acts 1:1; Luke 1:3.

The so-called "we" sections in Acts, Acts 16:10-17; 20:5-15; 21:1-18; 27:1–28:16 show that the author of Acts accompanied Paul on his travels.

The person Paul refers to as "dear friend Luke, the doctor," Colossians 4:14, and "fellow-worker," Philemon 24, combine to make Luke the most likely author of this Gospel.

Luke himself was not an eyewitness of Jesus' life, 1:1-4. From the New Testament we know that Luke was a companion and friend of Paul, 2 Timothy 4:11, and tradition says that he was a Gentile who died, unmarried, at the age of 84.

Date

The last event, Paul's house arrest, mentioned in Acts is probably at about AD 62. As Luke must have been written before Acts, it is reasonable to place the writing of Luke's Gospel between AD 60 and AD 65.

Setting

Luke addresses his Gospel to
Theophilus, 1:3, who was probably an
upper-class Gentile convert to
Christianity. We know nothing else
about him except that his name means
"loved of God."

Luke would have written his Gospel
for other people than just Theophilus.
Luke wrote for Gentiles and it has been
suggested that he especially had Roman
officials in mind.

Theme and purpose

Luke's reason for writing his Gospel is
stated quite clearly in his opening
words: "Many have undertaken to draw
up an account of the things that have
been fulfilled among us, just as they
were handed down to us by those who
from the first were eyewitnesses and
servants of the word. Therefore, since I
myself have carefully investigated
everything from the beginning, it
seemed good also to me to write an
orderly account for you, most excellent
Theophilus, so that you may know the
certainty of the things you have been
taught" Luke 1:1-4.

Special features of Luke's Gospel

1. Luke is a great story-teller.
2. Luke was an accomplished writer.
3. Luke wrote more about Jesus' early
   life and childhood than the other
   three Gospel writers.
4. Luke shows his interest in people

with his special reference to women,
children and social outcasts.
5. Luke wrote much about prayer.
6. Luke's Gospel is full of the theme
   of joy.
7. The Holy Spirit is one of Luke's
   special features.
8. Luke includes four beautiful hymns:
   a. the Magnificat of Mary, 1:46-55
   b. the Benedictus of Zacharias,
      1:67-79
   c. the Gloria in Excelsis of the
      heavenly host, 2:14
   d. the Nunc Dimittis of Simeon,
      2:28-32.

Learning from numbers

42 There are 42 different names and
titles given to Jesus in Luke's Gospel.

Overview

Luke and Acts make up 28% of the New
Testament, and Luke's writing adds up to
2,138 verses, exceeding Paul's 2,033
verses, which makes Luke the most
prolific writer in the New Testament.

OUTLINE	
1. Introduction and Jesus' birth and early years	1:1–4:13
2. Jesus and his ministry in Galilee	4:14–9:50
3. Jesus' visit to Jerusalem	9:51–19:27
4. Jesus' triumphal entry and last week in Jerusalem	19:28–23:56
5. Jesus' resurrection	24:1-53

The Gospel of John

KEYS TO UNLOCK JOHN	
KEY VERSE	*"Yet to all who received him, to those who believed in his name, he gave the right to become the children of God"* **1:12.**
KEY WORD	*Eternal life*
KEY PHRASE	*Whoever believes, 3:18, 36*
KEY PASSAGE	*Chapter 3, as it contains the most quoted verse in the Bible, 3:16*
KEY THOUGHT	*John's Gospel presents Jesus Christ as the Son of God and the two responses people made to him: faith and unbelief.*

Names and titles of God in John

- Father 1:18
- Spirit 4:24
- Holy Father 17:11
- Righteous Father 17:25

Name of book

This Gospel was originally entitled *Kata Ioannen*, "According to John," with the word "Gospel" being added later.

Author

There are numerous arguments that can be advanced in favor of the apostle John being the author of the Gospel which bears his name, which is the traditional view.

John's name does not appear in this Gospel, as he is always referred to as "the disciple whom Jesus loved" 13:23; 19:26; 20:2; 21:7, 20, 24. If John was

the author that would explain this, but as he was such a prominent member of the early church, the exclusion of his name from the whole Gospel would be strange.

The author was familiar with Jewish life.

a. He knew about the antipathy between Jews and Samaritans, 4:9.

b. He was knowledgeable about the geography of Palestine, saying that Bethany was some 15 stadia from Jerusalem, 11:18.

c. He was well-acquainted with Jewish customs, even the detail that circumcision had to be performed on the eighth day and that this took precedence over the Sabbath, 7:22.

Irenaeus, Clement of Alexandria, Theophilus of Antioch, Origen and Tertullian all say that John was the author of this Gospel.

Date

If John wrote his Gospel after the Synoptics, which is the traditional view, then the date of writing is about AD 85. However, if John wrote his Gospel independently of the Synoptics dates between AD 50 and AD 70 have been advanced.

Special features of John's Gospel

1. John's Gospel is the most theological of the Gospels and has more interpretation about events than the other Gospels.

2. John has no parables in his Gospel (but he does have allegories, the Good Shepherd, 10:1-8, and the True Vine, 15:1-6) and he does include 12 discourses which are unique to his Gospel.

3. John records seven "I am" statements made by Jesus:
   - "I am the bread of life," 6:35, 48
   - "I am the light of the world," 8:12; 9:5
   - "I am the door," 10:7, 9
   - "I am the good shepherd," 10:11, 14
   - "I am the resurrection, and the life," 11:25
   - "I am the way, the truth, and the life," 14:6
   - "I am the true vine," 15:1-5.

4. John states that Jesus' miracles were "miraculous signs" as they pointed to the life-giving results of believing in Jesus:
   - the changing water into wine at Cana, 2:1-11
   - the healing of the nobleman's son, 4:46-54
   - the healing of the paralytic, 5:1-16
   - the feeding of the 5,000, 6:1-13
   - Jesus walking on water, 6:16-21
   - sight given to the man born blind, 9:1-7
   - raising of Lazarus, 11:1-44.

Overview

John himself gives us his reason for writing this Gospel: "Jesus did many other miraculous signs in the presence of his disciples, which are not recorded in this book. But these are written that you may believe that Jesus is the Christ, the Son of God, and that by believing you may have life in his name" 20:30, 31.

OUTLINE	
1. The incarnation of the Son of God	1:1-18
2. The presentation of the Son of God	1:19–4:54
3. The opposition to the Son of God	5:1–12:50
4. The preparation of the disciples by the Son of God	13:1–17:26
5. The death and resurrection of the Son of God	18:1–21:25

An overview of the four Gospels

THE FOUR GOSPELS			
The Gospels are not biographies or even histories of the life of Jesus. Rather they are portraits of Israel's long-awaited Messiah who came in the person of Jesus Christ, as the Savior of the world. Strictly speaking the Gospels are not so much an exposition of the gospel, which is found in Paul's 13 letters, but they are more an account of the provision of the gospel for sinful people which is focused in the person and work of Jesus Christ.			
Matthew	*Mark*	*Luke*	*John*
PORTRAYAL OF CHRIST			
The prophesied King The Davidic King Lion-like	The obedient servant The Servant of the Lord Ox-like	The perfect Man The Son of Man Man-like	The divine Son The Word of God Eagle-like
OUTSTANDING FEATURE			
Sermons Outward Public Galilean Earthly	Miracles Outward Public Galilean Earthly	Parables Outward Public Galilean Earthly	Allegories Inward Private Judean Heavenly
ARRANGEMENT OF MATERIAL			
Topical	Chronological	Chronological	Topical
ORIGINAL AUDIENCE			
Jews	Romans	Greeks	Everyone
TONE			
Prophetic	Practical	Historical	Spiritual
UNIQUE MATERIAL			
42%	59%	7%	92%
QUOTATIONS FROM THE OLD TESTAMENT			
53	36	25	20
ALLUSIONS TO THE OLD TESTAMENT			
76	27	42	105
PERCENT OF WORDS SPOKEN BY JESUS			
60%	42%	50%	50%
NUMBER OF VERSES			
644	285	1149	866

Jesus' passion

JESUS' LAST WEEK

SATURDAY

• Supper at Bethany

SUNDAY

• Disciples bring Jesus a colt

• Jesus rides in humble triumph into Jerusalem

• Jesus returns to Bethany

MONDAY

• Jesus curses the fig tree

• Jesus cleanses the temple

TUESDAY

• Jesus' authority is challenged in the temple

• Parable of the two sons

• The dishonest manager

• The rejected stone

• The marriage feast

• Giving tribute money to Caesar

• Marriage and the resurrection

• The greatest commandment

• David's son and Lord

• Scribes and Pharisees denounced

• Jesus weeps over Jerusalem

• The poor widow's gift

• Greeks seek to speak with Jesus

• The Olivet discourse

• More parables:

• The fig tree

• The faithful and wicked servant

• The ten virgins

• The talents

• The sheep and the goats

• Judas plans Jesus' betrayal

WEDNESDAY

• A quiet day at Bethany

THURSDAY

• The Passover meal

• The Lord's Supper

• Jesus washes the disciples' feet

• Judas is identified as the traitor

• The upper room discourse

• Jesus' high priestly prayer

• Jesus prays in Gethsemane

• Jesus is betrayed

• Jesus is arrested

• Peter cuts off Malchus' ear

FRIDAY

• Jesus on trial before Annas

• Jesus on trial before Caiaphas

• Jesus on trial before Sanhedrin

• Jesus declares himself to be the Messiah

• Peter denies Jesus three times

• Jesus is mocked

• Jesus on trial before Pilate

• Jesus on trial before Herod

• Jesus on trial before Pilate again

• Pilate hands Jesus over to the Jews

• Judas commits suicide

ORDER OF EVENTS OF JESUS' CRUCIFIXION

• Jesus taken to Golgotha/Calvary

• Offered a drugged drink

• First three hours

• 9.00–12.00am

• Jesus is crucified

• Jesus' first cry, "Father, forgive…"

• Jesus' clothes are gambled over

• Jesus' is mocked

• The two thieves mock Jesus

• But one thief believes in Jesus

• Jesus' second cry, "Today you will be with me…"

• Jesus' third cry, "Dear woman, here is your son…"

• Second three hours

• 12.00–3.00pm

• Darkness over the land

• Jesus' fourth cry, "My God, my God…"

• Jesus' fifth cry, "I am thirsty"

• Jesus' sixth cry, "It is finished"

• Jesus' seventh cry, "Father, into your hands…"

• Supernatural events follow Jesus' death

• Darkness, earthquake, temple curtain torn in two

• Body of Jesus buried in Joseph's tomb

Acts

KEYS TO UNLOCK ACTS	
KEY VERSE	*"But you will receive power when the Holy Spirit comes on you; and you will be my witnesses in Jerusalem, and in all Judea and Samaria, and to the ends of the earth" 1:8.*
KEY WORD	*Witness*
KEY PHRASE	*The gift my Father promised, 1:4*
KEY PASSAGE	*Chapter 2, the Day of Pentecost and the coming of the Holy Spirit*
KEY THOUGHT	*"We must obey God rather than men!" 5:29.*

Names and titles of the Holy Spirit in Acts

- Holy Spirit 1:2
- The gift my Father promised 1:4
- Spirit 2:4
- The Spirit of the Lord 5:9

Name of book

All known Greek manuscripts entitle this book as *Praxeis*, "Acts," or with the extended title of "The Acts of the Apostles." *Praxeis* was often used in Greek literature to summarize the deeds of outstanding men. While it is true that Jesus' apostles are mentioned as groups in Acts, the book may also be divided into:

- The acts of Peter, 1–12
- The acts of Paul, 13–28

This book could also be correctly entitled, "The Acts of the Holy Spirit."

Author

Dr Luke wrote this book to a certain Theophilus, 1:1. See also *The Gospel of Luke, Author*, p 96. From within the book of Acts it is clear that the writer of Acts was Paul's companion for many of the events described in this book.

Date

The mid-sixties. This would be a little after the last event recorded in Acts.

Theme and purpose

Luke sets the scene for the scope of his second book in the opening verses: "He said to them: 'It is not for you to know the times or dates the Father has set by his own authority. But you will receive power when the Holy Spirit comes on you; and you will be my witnesses in Jerusalem, and in all Judea and Samaria, and to the ends of the earth'" 1:7, 8.

Special features of Luke's Gospel

1. Luke is meticulously accurate and all the relevant archaeological discoveries confirm this. He mentions nearly 80 geographical locations and over 100 people by name.
2. Luke records a number of conversions to Christ in Acts:
   - The Ethiopian official, 8:30
   - Saul of Tarsus, 9:1-19
   - Lydia, 16:14
   - The Philippian jailer, 16:29, 30.
3. Luke records a number of defenses

made on behalf of Christianity in Acts, which were made in front of both Jews, 4:8-12, and Gentiles, 25:8-11.

4. Acts is a book of transitions:
   - From the Gospels to the Letters of the New Testament
   - From law to grace
   - From Jews alone to Jews and Gentiles.

5. Luke records 24 speeches and sermons which give us an authentic record of the content and apologetic nature of the way the first Christian preachers communicated with a wide variety of people.

6. As in his Gospel, Luke lays a great emphasis on prayer in Acts. He records:
   - a prayer for unity, 1:14
   - a prayer to know God's will in

church appointments, 1:24
   - a prayer prayed at a regular time for prayer, 3:1
   - prayer linked to studying God's Word, 6:4
   - prayer for new Christians, 8:15
   - prayer for missionaries, 13:2-4
   - prayer for Christians to help spread the gospel, 16:9
   - prayer when facing trials, 16:25
   - prayer for church leaders, 21:4, 5.

Overview

Luke's second volume, Acts, is a bridge between the four Gospels and the life of the Christian church after the death, resurrection, and ascension of Jesus. Acts spans 30 years, and chronicles the dynamic growth of Christianity, from the birth of the church at Pentecost in Jerusalem, the religious capital of the Jewish people, to the apostle Paul gossiping the gospel during his two-year house arrest in Rome, the capital of the civilized world.

OUTLINE	
1. The beginning of the church	1:1–2:47
2. The gospel in Jerusalem	3:1–7:60
3. The gospel spreads to Samaria, Joppa, Caesarea, and Antioch	8:1–12:25
4. Paul's three missionary journeys	13:1–21:16
5. Paul's arrest and journey to Rome	21:17–28:31

5 THE BIBLE, BOOK BY BOOK: THE NEW TESTAMENT, ROMANS THRU' REVELATION

CONTENTS

Introduction

As we come to study the letters of the New Testament you may feel that you wish to follow George Whitefield's approach to Bible study, as he recorded it in his *Journal*: "I began to read the holy scriptures upon my knees, laying aside all other books, and praying over, if possible, every line and word. This proved meat indeed and drink to my soul. I daily received fresh life, light and power from above."

As all the New Testament letters were originally letters, try treating them as letters. Read them right through from beginning to end, as you would with any other letter. Read them aloud, as they would have been read in the first century. See what you glean from this way of approaching each New Testament letter before you study each one with the aid of the following 27 studies.

Romans

KEYS TO UNLOCK ROMANS	
KEY VERSE	*"I am not ashamed of the gospel because it is the power of God for the salvation of everyone who believes: first the Jew, then for the Gentiles" 1:16.*
KEY WORD	*Righteousness*
KEY PHRASE	*In Christ*
KEY PASSAGE	*Chapters 6–8, basic teaching on the spiritual life*
KEY THOUGHT	*It is possible to approach God clothed in Jesus' righteousness.*

Names and titles of God in Romans

- Our Father 1:7
- Creator 1:25
- One God 3:30
- Lord 4:8
- Abba, Father 8:15
- The living God 9:26
- The Lord Almighty 9:29
- Lord of all 10:12
- God of peace 16:20
- Everlasting God 16:26
- The only wise God 16:27

Name of letter

The title *Pros Romaious*, "To the Romans," has been linked with this letter almost from the time when it was first known about.

Author

The early church with one voice agreed that this letter was written by the apostle Paul. Its vocabulary, style, theological development, and even logic, are consistent with Paul's other letters. This letter also has historical references which fit in with the parts of Paul's life which we know about.

Paul dictated nearly all his letters. For Romans his secretary was Tertius, 16:22.

Date

Paul wrote this letter towards the end of his third missionary tour in AD 57.

Paul probably wrote Romans from Corinth. At the end of this letter Paul refers to Phoebe who lived six miles away from Corinth, at Cenchrea; to his host Gaius, who probably came from Corinth, see Romans 16:23 and 1 Corinthians 1:14; and to Erastus, who may well have also come from Corinth, see 16:23 and 2 Timothy 4:20.

Setting

Paul is writing what has been called "the Gospel According to Paul" to the Christians at Rome who were mainly Gentiles by background.

Theme and purpose

Romans is the most formal of all Paul's letters and it reads more like a treatise than a letter. Paul's main theme in this letter centers round God's plan of salvation for humankind which results in Jew and Gentile alike being made righteous in God's sight. This righteousness which comes from God includes justification by faith, deals with humankind's guilt, and is the basis for

any Christian's subsequent sanctification and eternal security. Paul explains that Jesus' death and resurrection is the basis for a Christian's:

- redemption
- justification
- reconciliation
- salvation
- glorification.

Praise given to Romans

"The most profound book in existence." *Samuel Taylor Coleridge*

"The cathedral of the Christian faith." *Bible commentator Godet*

"This letter is the heart of the New Testament and the very purest gospel. It can never be read or pondered too much, and the more it is dealt with the more precious it becomes, and the better it tastes." *Martin Luther*

Few would disagree that Paul's letter to the Romans has been more influential in the Christian church than any other letter.

Special features of Romans
Learning from numbers
78 Paul explains how Christians are no longer under the law. This word "law" Paul refers to 78 times in this letter. **66** The word "righteousness" comes 66 times in Romans. **60** and **62** Paul explains how people need the gospel because of sin, which he mentions 60 times. He points his readers to the necessity of having faith, in Christ. Paul mentions "faith" 62 times in this letter.

Overview
In Romans Paul explains:

1. The revelation of the righteousness of God, 1–8
2. The vindication of the righteousness of God, 9–11
3. The application of the righteousness of God, 12–16.

OUTLINE		
1.	Greetings: and this sinful world needs the gospel	1:1–3:20
2.	God's plan of salvation	3:21–5:21
3.	The power of the gospel	6:1–8:39
4.	How the gospel applies to Jews	9:1–11:36
5.	How the gospel transforms the believer	12:1–15:33
6.	Greetings	16:1–27

1 Corinthians

KEYS TO UNLOCK 1 CORINTHIANS	
KEY VERSE	*"No, we speak of God's secret wisdom, a wisdom that has been hidden and that God destined for our glory before time began"* 1:7.
KEY WORD	*Wisdom*
KEY PHRASE	*The greatest…is love*
KEY PASSAGE	*Chapter 15, and its teaching about resurrection*
KEY THOUGHT	*Paul explains how Christian principles apply to the questions the Christians in Corinth have asked him.*

Names and titles of the Holy Spirit in 1 Corinthians

- His [God's] Spirit 2:10
- The Spirit 2:10
- The Spirit of God 2:11
- Holy Spirit 2:13
- The Spirit of our God 6:11

Name of letter

The most ancient title of this letter is *Pros Korinthious A*, meaning "First to the Corinthians." The "A" must have been a later addition to distinguish it from 2 Corinthians.

Author

As early as AD 96, when Clement of Rome wrote to the Christians at Corinth he quoted part of 1 Corinthians to them. The letter itself, 1:1, 2 and 16:21, states that Paul wrote it. Few have ever questioned Paul's authorship of 1 Corinthians.

Date

While Paul was occupied for three years preaching and teaching in Ephesus, during his third missionary tour, see 16:5-9 and Acts 20:31, he wrote this letter. The date was AD 55.

Setting

In many way Corinth claimed to be the leading city in Greece of its day, with a quarter of a million free persons, and nearly twice as many slaves.

It was a great commercial center and boasted about being a very religious place, having at least 12 temples in Paul's day. But the city of Corinth had the worst of all possible reputations because of its immorality. In the Temple

of Aphrodite worshipers of the goddess of love were allowed to freely make use of the 1,000 Hieroduli (so-called "sacred" prostitutes.) Corinth became a byword for license and evil practice. A new word was even coined to describe Corinth. *Korinthiazomai* ("to act like a Corinthian") became a synonym for prostitution.

Theme and purpose

The new Christian converts had asked Paul a set of questions. Reading 1 Corinthians is like listening to just one end of a telephone conversation, as one reads about Paul's divinely inspired advice to these spiritually gifted, yet very immature Christians who had grown up knowing only the ways of worldly Corinth.

Paul had heard by word of mouth that some of the Corinthian Christians were indulging in some very godless practices. Paul writes to correct their bad behavior and their mistaken beliefs by telling them:

- to heal the divisions in the church, 1:10–4:21;
- not to indulge in incest, 5:1-8. "It is actually reported that there is sexual immorality among you, and of a kind that does not occur even among pagans. A man has his father's wife" 5:1;
- to separate from immoral believers, 5:9-13;
- not to take a fellow-Christian to court, 6:1-11;

- not to indulge in sexual immorality, 6:12-20;
- not to abuse the Lord's Supper, 11:17-34;
- not to entertain false teaching about the resurrection, chapter 15.

Special features of 1 Corinthians

Paul introduces the topics the Corinthians have asked him about in a letter with the words "Now for the matters you wrote about," or "Now about."

1. Now about your questions about marriage: 7:1-40
2. Now about your questions about things offered to idols: 8:1–11:1
3. Now about your questions about exercising spiritual gifts: 12:1–14:40
4. Now about your questions about the collection for God's people: 16:1-4

OUTLINE	
1. Introduction	1:1-9
2. Divisions in the Corinthian church	1:10–4:21
3. Moral disorders in the Corinthian church	5–11
4. Spiritual gifts and their misuse	12:1–14:40
5. Teaching about the resurrection	15:1-58
6. Conclusion	16:1-24

2 Corinthians

KEYS TO UNLOCK 2 CORINTHIANS	
KEY VERSE	*"Therefore, if anyone is in Christ, he is a new creation; the old has gone, the new has come!" 5:17.*
KEY WORD	*Glory*
KEY PHRASE	*The things that mark an apostle, 12:12*
KEY PASSAGE	*Chapters 8–9, with the fullest teaching in the New Testament about stewardship*
KEY THOUGHT	*Paul defends his own ministry in the teeth of strong attacks made against him from some members of the Corinthian church.*

Names and titles of the Holy Spirit in 2 Corinthians

- The Spirit 1:22
- The Spirit of the living God 3:3
- The Lord 3:17
- The Spirit of the Lord 3:17
- Holy Spirit 6:6

Name of letter

To distinguish this letter from 1 Corinthians it was given the title *Pros Korinthious B*, the "Second to the Corinthians." The *A* and the *B* were later additions.

Author

This letter claims to be by Paul, 1:1; 10:1, and has more autobiographical information about the apostle Paul than any of his other letters.

Date

Paul was in Corinth when Gallio was proconsul in Achaia, Acts 18:12, and this can be dated to AD 51 or 52. This places the writing of 1 Corinthians and 2 Corinthians at AD 55. 2 Corinthians 2:13 and 7:5 show that he wrote it from Macedonia.

Setting

To appreciate the contents of 2 Corinthians it helps to know about the story behind the letter.

1. Paul had been used by God to found the church at Corinth, Acts 18:1-17.
2. Paul had claimed to be an apostle, 1 Corinthians 9:1, and emphasizes this in 2 Corinthians 1:1, "Paul, an apostle of Christ Jesus by the will of God."
3. False apostles had infiltrated themselves into the Corinthian church, 11:12-15.

4. These "super-apostles" 11:5, were dangerous as they taught a different gospel, 11:12-15, and attacked Paul's authority.
5. This caused turmoil among the Christians, some of whom ignored Paul's advice in 1 Corinthians.
6. So Paul paid them a second visit, a very painful one, 2:1.
7. The "super-apostles" derided Paul, 10:10.
8. So Paul then sent Titus to Corinth with a very severe letter, 7:5-13.
9. The Corinthian Christians then repented and Titus brought this encouraging news back to Paul, 7:6, 7.
10. 2 Corinthians is like a running commentary on these events.

Theme and purpose

1. The main purpose behind 2 Corinthians was to tell the Christians at Corinth how pleased Paul was with their change of mind.
2. 2 Corinthians warns the Corinthians not to be too harsh on those with whom they had disagreed, 2:5-11.
3. Paul underlines some of the teaching he had already given in 1 Corinthians. Compare 6:14, "Do not be yoked together with unbelievers," with 1 Corinthians 6:15-20.
4. Paul exposes the false teachers, 11:1-5.

5. Paul reminds the Corinthians about the collection for the poor Christian in Jerusalem, and he asks them now to send their money by Titus, 9:1-5.

Special feature of 2 Corinthians
In 2 Corinthians Jesus is presented as the believer's:

- comfort, 1:5
- triumph, 2:14
- Lord, 4:5
- light, 4:6
- Judge, 5:10
- reconciliation, 5:19
- substitute, 5:21
- gift, 9:15
- owner, 10:7
- power, 12:9.

Learning from numbers
9 Paul clearly valued Titus, 2:13; 8:23, and he mentions Titus nine times in the letter. Titus took Paul's "severe" letter and 2 Corinthians to the Corinthian Christians. He also shared in Paul's concern for them.

OUTLINE	
1. Greetings	1:1-11
2. Paul's plea to the Corinthians	1:12–3:18
3. Paul's explanation about his own ministry	4:1–7:16
4. The offering for the Christians in Judea	8:1–9:15
5. Paul defends his apostleship	10:1–13:14

Galatians

KEYS TO UNLOCK GALATIANS	
KEY VERSE	*"...a man is not justified by observing the law, but by faith in Jesus Christ. So we, too, have put our faith in Christ Jesus that we may be justified by faith in Christ and not by observing the law, because by observing the law no one will be justified" 2:16.*
KEY WORD	*Freedom*
KEY PHRASE	*Stand firm, 5:1*
KEY PASSAGE	*Chapter 3, with its teaching about justification by faith*
KEY THOUGHT	*Paul wrote this letter to bring back to the true Christian faith those who had been misled by false teachers.*

Names and titles of God in Galatians

- Father 1:1
- Mediator 3:20
- *Abba*, Father 4:6

Name of letter

This book was called *Pros Galatas*, "To the Galatians." It is the only Pauline letter that is specifically addressed to a number of churches: "To the churches in Galatia" 1:2.

Author

Paul is identified as the author of this letter in 1:1 and 6:11 and this has rarely been questioned.

"Paul, an aportle... see what large letters I use..."

Date

When this letter was written hinges on to whom the letter was written. If it was written to South Galatia, as most scholars now hold, it would be Paul's first letter, written in about AD 48. If it was written to North Galatia it would have been written about eight or nine years later.

Theme and purpose

Justification by faith, apart from deeds done under the Law, is the central theme of this urgent letter.

1. In the first two chapters Paul defends his own apostolic authority because this gives weight to his teaching about the message of the gospel.
2. In chapters three and four Paul gives a theological defense about justification by faith and refutes the false teachers who taught about justification by the law.
3. In the last two chapters Paul reminds his readers that freedom from the law does not mean that they can live in a lawless way.

Special features of Galatians

In Galatians Paul shows a number of ways in which the Holy Spirit relates to the believer:

- He is promised, 3:14.
- He is sent by God, 4:6.
- He is active in a believer's life, 3:5.
- He is received by faith, 3:2.

- He lives in a believer's heart, 4:6.
- He initiates a believer's life with Jesus, 3:3.
- He leads, 5:18.
- He helps believers not to gratify the desires of the sinful nature, 5:16.
- He bears fruit, 5:22-24.
- He enables believers to reap eternal life, 6:8.

Martin Luther and Galatians

Martin Luther was helped greatly in his own Christian life by Galatians. In order to pass on the message of Galatians to his students he placed the following 50 statements at the beginning of his commentary on Galatians.

Fifty Inconveniences That Arise out of Man's Own Righteousness Coming from Works, Extracted from Paul's Letter to the Galatians

Chapter 1

1. To bring people from the calling of grace.
2. To receive another gospel.
3. To trouble the minds of the faithful.
4. To pervert the gospel of Christ.
5. To be accursed.
6. To obey human traditions.
7. To please humankind.
8. Not to be the servant of Christ.
9. To be built on humans, and not on God.
10. That the most excellent righteousness of the law is nothing.
11. To destroy the church of God.

Chapter 2

12. To teach people to be justified by works is to teach them to be justified by impossibility.

13. To make the righteous in Christ into sinners.
14. To make Christ a minister of sin.
15. To build up sin again, when it is destroyed.
16. To be made a transgressor.
17. To reject the grace of God.
18. To judge that Christ died in vain.

Chapter 3

19. To become foolish Galatians.
20. To be bewitched.
21. Not to listen to the truth.
22. To crucify Christ again.
23. To hold that the Spirit is received by performing deeds.
24. To forsake the Spirit and to end in the flesh.
25. To be under the curse.
26. To set human testimony above God's testimony.
27. To make sin abound.
28. To be enclosed by sin.
29. To serve beggarly ceremonies.

Chapter 4

30. That the gospel is preached in vain.
31. That everything the faithful do or permit is in vain.
32. To be made a servant and the son of the slave woman.
33. To be cast out of inheritance, together with the son of the slave woman.
34. That Christ brings no benefit.
35. That we are debtors to fulfill the whole law.

Chapter 5

36. To be separate from Christ.
37. To fall from grace.
38. To be hindered from doing good.
39. To be convinced about the teaching of good deeds does not come from God.
40. To have the yeast of corruption.
41. To take a view about this which is different from the Lord's view.
42. To throw people into confusion.
43. That this doctrine is thought to be one of the works of the flesh.

Chapter 6

44. To think yourself to be something when you are nothing.
45. To glory in others rather than in God.
46. To please people in an unspiritual way.
47. To hate being persecuted for the sake of the cross.
48. Not to keep the law itself.
49. To glory in the master and teacher of unspiritual things.
50. That nothing helps at all, and whatever a person does is in vain.

Overview
The false teachers Paul was dealing with were known as "Judaizers" who claimed to follow Jesus, but said that any non-Jew who became a Christian must live according to the requirements of the Mosaic Law, 1:7; 4:17, 21; 5:2-12; 6:12-13. "You who want to be under the law" 4:21.

Ephesians

KEYS TO UNLOCK EPHESIANS	
KEY VERSE	*"Praise be to the God and Father of our Lord Jesus Christ, who has blessed us in the heavenly realms with every spiritual blessing in Christ" 1:3.*
KEY WORD	*Fullness*
KEY PHRASE	*In Christ, with Christ*
KEY PASSAGE	*Chapter 1, with its description of a believer in Christ*
KEY THOUGHT	*The purpose of this letter is to exalt the name of Jesus Christ.*

Names and titles of God in Ephesians

- Father 1:2
- God of our Lord Jesus Christ 1:17
- Father of glory 1:17

Name of letter

The traditional title of this letter is *Pros Ephesious*, "To the Ephesians." However, many ancient manuscripts omit the words *en Epheso*, "in Ephesus," from 1:1. Because of this it has been suggested that this letter may have been intended to be a circular letter written for the benefit of different Christian groups in the locality of Ephesus. This might account for the letter not starting with a personal greeting.

Author

This letter states that its author is Paul, 1:1; 3:1, and there is no good reason to doubt this.

Date

Paul probably wrote Ephesians while he was in prison in Rome in AD 60.

Setting

Paul had spent three years preaching and teaching in Ephesus, Acts 19:8, 10; 20:31. It was the commercial center of Asia Minor, given over to pagan worship which focused on Diana's temple (Artemis). The practice of magic flourished.

Theme and purpose

This letter was not written to correct any specific defect or to solve any one problem, but to encourage Christians to become spiritually mature in Jesus. After this doctrinal teaching, Paul moved on to apply this to everyday living. Paul ends with a description of the armor Christians must use if they are to withstand Satan's constant attacks.

OUTLINE		
1.	Introduction	1:1-2
2.	The Christian's inheritance	1:3–2:22
3.	The revealing of a mystery	3:1-21
4.	The nature of the church	4:1-32
5.	Responsibilities at home and at work	5:1–6:9
6.	Facing the enemy	6:10-24

Ephesians and Colossians compared

There are some remarkable similarities between Ephesians and Colossians

1. The same words and expressions occur in both letters.
2. Some passages are identical in thought and language.
3. Other passages have the same thought, though the expression varies.
4. In some passages different topics follow each other in the same order.

There are some striking points of difference between Ephesians and Colossians

1. While the letter to the Colossians has every indication of having been written to a particular congregation, and in reference to their peculiar circumstances, the absence of these features is the most remarkable characteristic of the letter to the Ephesians.
2. In the letter to the Ephesians the doctrinal element prevails over the practical; in the letter to the Colossians it is just the reverse.
3. The main object of the letter to the Colossians is to warn the church against hollow and deceptive philosophy. There is no talk of this in Ephesians, whose purpose is to focus on the glories of the plan of redemption as they embrace both Jews and Gentiles and are intended to be the medium for the manifestation of the grace and wisdom of God to all intelligent creatures.

4. There are, therefore, topics discussed in the one letter to which nothing corresponds in the other.
5. The order of subjects, except in the case of some particular exhortations, is entirely different in the two letters.
6. The letter to the Ephesians has much greater unity than that to the Colossians. This evidently arose from the different purposes for which they were written.

The two letters are evidently independent of one another

Each is a self-contained unit. In each, one topic flows naturally from another, the association of ideas in every case being clearly indicated.

Conclusion

All these characteristics of similarity, dissimilarity, and mutual independence are naturally accounted for on the assumption that the two letters were written at the same time – one for a particular congregation, the other for a particular group of readers.

Philippians

KEYS TO UNLOCK PHILIPPIANS	
KEY VERSE	*"Your attitude should be the same as that of Christ Jesus" 2:5.*
KEY WORD	*Joy, rejoice*
KEY PHRASE	*Rejoice in the Lord*
KEY PASSAGE	*Chapter 2, with its portrait of the humility of Jesus*
KEY THOUGHT	*Paul writes about the God-given joy and peace which should be experienced by his Christian friends at Philippi.*

Names and titles of God in Philippians

- Father 1:2
- God of peace 4:9

Name of letter

This letter is called *Pros Philippesioius*, "To the Philippians." The church at Philippi in Macedonia was the first Christian church to be founded on European soil.

Author

This letter itself claims to be written by Paul, 1:1, and there are many personal references in it which confirm this, 1:12-20; 2:19-24. "I hope… to send Timothy to you soon" 1:19.

Date

Paul is clearly in prison when he wrote this letter, "I am in chains," 1:13. This prison was most probably in Rome, from where Paul would have written this letter in about AD 61.

Special features of Philippians

1. Paul shows that he has a special affection for the Christians who lived in Philippi. The Christians there were a source of joy and encouragement to him, 1:3-5.
2. 2:5-11 may have been part of an early Christian hymn. It is one of the most outstanding passages about Jesus in the New Testament. Condensed into these seven verses is teaching about Jesus' pre-existence, incarnation, humiliation and exultation.
3. Paul warns his friends about the pernicious teaching of the legalists, whom he calls "dogs," 3:2, which was their name for Gentiles.

Learning from numbers

16 The outstanding characteristic of this letter is the theme of joy and of rejoicing in Jesus. Paul uses the word "joy" 16 times in Philippians.

"Rejoice the Lord always. I will say it again: Rejoice!" 4:4

"I rejoice greatly in the Lord that at last you have renewed your concern for me" 4:10.

OUTLINE		
1.	Find joy in suffering	1:1-30
2.	Find joy in service	2:1-30
3.	Find joy in Jesus	3:1-21
4.	Find joy and contentment	4:1-21

Philippians and Romans: parallel passages

PARALLEL PASSAGES	
Philippians has more close parallels with Romans than any other Pauline letter.	
Philippians	**Romans**
1 I thank my God every time I remember you. In all my prayers for all of you…all of you share in God's grace with me. God can testify how I long for you all with the affection of Christ Jesus. *Philippians 1:3, 4, 7, 8*	First, I thank God through Jesus Christ for all of you…God…is my witness how constantly I remember you in my prayers at all times; and I pray…I long to see you so that I may impart some spiritual gift to make you strong. *Romans 1:8-11*
2 That you may be able to discern what is best. *Philippians 1:10*	You…approve of what is superior. *Romans 2:18*
3 [He] became obedient to death… Therefore God exalted him to the highest place…that at the name of Jesus every knee should bow, in heaven and on earth and under the earth, and every tongue confess that Jesus Christ is Lord. *Phillippians 2:8, 9 10, 11*	For this very reason, Christ died and returned to life so that he might be the Lord of both the dead and the living…It is written: "'As surely as I live,' says the Lord, 'every knee will bow before me; every tongue will confess to God.'" (Isaiah 45:23) *Romans 14:9, 11*
4 Being like-minded, having the same love, being one in spirit and purpose. Do nothing out of selfish ambition or vain conceit, but in humility consider others better than yourselves. *Philippians 2:2-4*	Live in harmony with one another. Do not be proud…Do not be conceited…live at peace with everyone. Do not take revenge. *Romans 12:16-19* Honor one another above yourselves. *Romans 12:10*

	Philippians	Romans
5	For it is we who are the circumcision, we who worship by the Spirit of God, who glory in Christ Jesus... *Philippians 3:3* If anyone else thinks he has reasons to put confidence in the flesh, I have more:...of the people of Israel, of the tribe of Benjamin. *Philippians 3: 4, 5*	A man is not a Jew if he is only one outwardly...circumcision of the heart. *Romans 2:28, 29* God, whom I serve with my whole heart. *Romans 1:9* Rejoice in God through our Lord Jesus Christ. *Romans 1:11* I am an Israelite myself, a descendant of Abraham, from the tribe of Benjamin. *Romans 1:11*
6	Becoming like him in his death, and so, somehow, to attain to the resurrection from the dead. *Philippians 3:10, 11* That they will be like his glorious body. *Philippians 3:21*	They did not know the righteousness that comes from God and sought to establish their own [righteousness]. *Romans 10:3* Pursued a law of righteousness...not by faith but as if it were by works. *Romans 9:31, 32* If we have been united with him in his death, we will certainly also be united with him in his resurrection. *Romans 6:5* For those God foreknew he also predestined to be conformed to the likeness of his Son. *Romans 8:29*
7	Their destiny is destruction, their god is their stomach. *Philippians 3:19*	Those things result in death! *Romans 6:21* Such people are not serving our Lord Christ, but their own appetites. *Romans 16:18*
8	I have received from Epaphroditus the gifts you sent. They are a fragrant offering, an acceptable sacrifice, pleasing to God. *Philippians 4:18*	Offer your bodies as living sacrifices, holy and pleasing to God. *Romans 12:1*

Colossians

KEYS TO UNLOCK COLOSSIANS	
KEY VERSE	*"For in Christ all the fullness of the Deity lives in bodily form"* 2:9.
KEY WORD	*Christ*
KEY PHRASE	*Raised with Christ*
KEY PASSAGE	*Chapter 1, Jesus living in his followers*
KEY THOUGHT	*Christ is preeminent.*

Names and titles of God in Colossians

- Father 1:2
- Father of our Lord Jesus Christ 1:3

Name of letter

This letter became known as *Pros Kolossaeis*, "To the Colossians," because 1:2 states, "To the holy and faithful brothers in Christ at Colossae." Paul says that he wanted this letter also to be read by the Christians at neighboring Laodicea, 4:16.

Author

The letter itself states that Paul was its author, 1:1, 23: 4:18. "I, Paul, write this greeting in my own hand" 4:18. In addition to this the personal details and close parallels with Ephesians and Philemon confirm the Pauline authorship of this letter.

Date

It is most likely that Paul wrote this letter during his two-year house arrest in Rome, Acts 28:16-31, in AD 60.

Setting

Paul writes to the church at Colossae, a town in Asia Minor to the east of Ephesus. Paul did not found the church but now seeks to oppose the heretical teaching which has infiltrated in that church fellowship.

Theme and purpose

The so-called Colossian heresy consisted of:

- keeping ceremonial rules linked to eating and drinking and observing festivals, 2:16, 17;
- angel worship, 2:18;
- adopting ascetic practices, 2:21;
- relying on human traditions, 2:4, 8;
- boasting that they possessed secret knowledge, like the Gnostics, 2:18, 22, 23;
- effectively reducing the preeminence of Jesus, see 1:15-20; 2:2–3:9.

Special feature of Colossians

Colossians contrasts false and genuine wisdom. Paul makes reference to three words concerning wisdom:

1. Wisdom, 1:9, 28; 2:3; 3:16
2. Understanding, 1:9; 22
3. Knowledge, 1:9, 10; 2:3.

Paul makes use of the language of his opponents and then translates it into a higher plane. The false teachers:

1. propose a "philosophy," but it was only an empty deceit, only a plausible display of false reasoning, 2:4, 8;

2. pretended "wisdom," but it was merely a profession, not a reality, 2:23. Against these pretensions Paul sets the true wisdom of the gospel which he is never tired of emphasizing, 1:9, 28; 3:16. Paul argues that the true wisdom is essentially spiritual and yet essentially definite, while false wisdom is speculative, vague and dreamy, 2:4, 18;

3. had their rites of initiation. Paul contrasts these with the one universal, all-embracing mystery, 1:26, 27; 2:2; 4:3, that knowledge of God in Jesus. This mystery is complete in itself. It contains "all the treasures of wisdom and knowledge" 2:3. In addition to this, it is offered to everyone, and not to a select few. Though it was once hidden, its revelation is now unrestricted, except to those who deliberately disobey God.

Overview

To counter the Colossian heresy Paul concentrates on the cosmic Jesus, who is:

- "the head over every power and authority," 2:10
- the Lord of creation, 1:16, 17
- the Author of reconciliation, 1:20-22
- the basis for a believer's hope, 1:5, 23, 27
- the source of the believer's power for new life, 1:11, 29
- the head of the Church, 1:18.

Ephesians and Colossians

The letter to the Ephesians and the letter to the Colossians can be compared and contrasted in several ways. (See also p 116.)

Ephesians

Written in prison, delivered by Tychicus. Stresses wisdom, knowledge, fullness, mystery. Similar passages:

1. 1:7	4. 1:18
2. 1:10	5. 1:19, 20
3. 1:15-17	6. 1:21-23

Emphasizes the church as the body of Christ. General, universal. Specific, local.

Colossians

Written in prison, delivered by Tychicus. Stresses wisdom, knowledge, fullness, mystery. Similar passages:

1. 1:4	4. 1:27
2. 1:20	5. 2:12
3. 1:3, 4	6. 1:16-19

Emphasizes the church as the body of Christ. Emphasizes Christ as the Head of the church. Reflective, quiet. Spiritual conflict.

OUTLINE	
1. Introduction	1:1-8
2. Jesus' nature and work	1:9–2:19
3. New life in Jesus	2:20–4:6
4. Closing remarks and greetings	4:7-18

1 Thessalonians

KEYS TO UNLOCK 1 THESSALONIANS	
KEY VERSE	*"For the Lord himself will come down from heaven, with a loud command, with the voice of the archangel and with the trumpet call of God, and the dead in Christ will rise first"* 4:16.
KEY WORD	*Sanctified*
KEY PHRASE	*In Christ*
KEY PASSAGE	*Chapter 4, and its teaching about the coming of the Lord*
KEY THOUGHT	*When will Jesus return again?*

Names and titles of God in 1 Thessalonians

- Father 1:1
- Living and true God 1:9
- God of peace 5:23

Name of letter

As this was the first of two letters Paul wrote to the Thessalonians it was called, *Pros Thessalonikeis A*, the "First to the Thessalonians."

Author

The letter itself claims to be written by Paul, 1:1; 2:18. In addition to this, the letter contains some of Paul's well-known characteristics, 3:1-2, 8-11, which tie in with Acts 15:36 and 2 Corinthians 11:28. Also some of the allusions made in the letter by the writer exactly fit in with Paul's life as Luke recorded it in Acts. See 2:14-16; Acts 17:5-10; 3:6; 17:16. There is overwhelming internal and external evidence that the apostle Paul wrote 1 Thessalonians.

Date

The most probable date of the writing of this letter, AD 51, has been confirmed by an inscription uncovered at Delphi, Greece, which dates the time that Gallio was proconsul to AD 51–52. From Acts 18:12-17 it is clear that Paul was there at that time.

With the possible exception of Galatians, this is the earliest of Paul's surviving letters.

Overview

1. Paul wanted to say how glad he was that these new Christians had survived under persecution.
2. Paul defends himself against unjust attacks from some Jews.
3. Paul outlines how Christians are to resist temptaion.
4. Paul teaches about Jesus' coming.
5. Paul teaches about spiritual leaders and worship.

OUTLINE	
1. Greetings and exhortations to Christian conduct	1:1–2:20
2. Paul's joy over Timothy's report	3:1-13
3. Moral questions	4:1-12
4. Jesus' coming and the Day of the Lord	4:13–5:29

2 Thessalonians

KEYS TO UNLOCK 2 THESSALONIANS	
KEY VERSE	*"But we ought always to thank God for you, brothers loved by the Lord, because from the beginning God chose you to be saved through the sanctifying work of the Spirit and through belief in the truth" 2:13.*
KEY WORD	*Coming*
KEY PHRASE	*The lawless one*
KEY PASSAGE	*Chapter 2, which corrects the false idea that the day of the Lord had already come*
KEY THOUGHT	*Wait and work until Jesus comes.*

Names and titles of God in 2 Thessalonians

- Father 1:1
- Lord of peace 3:16

Name of letter

Since this was the second letter in Paul's Thessalonian correspondence this was entitled *Pros Thessalonikeis B*, the "Second to the Thessalonians."

Author

This letter states that it was written by the apostle Paul, 1:1; 3:17, and the vocabulary, style, and theological content of the letter support this.

Date

This letter appears to have been written not very many months after 1 Thessalonians, which dates it to AD 51 or 52. After Silas and Timothy had delivered 1 Thessalonians and had returned to the apostle, Paul probably wrote 2 Thessalonians, from Corinth.

Theme and purpose

This is the shortest of Paul's letters to churches. However, it gives crucial information about the end times. Paul teaches that before Jesus returns, evil will reach a high point under the leadership of a mysterious figure called "The Wicked One," who will be implacably opposed to Jesus.

Special features of 2 Thessalonians

In 3:17, Paul ends this letter with a greeting in his own handwriting. "I, Paul, write this greeting in my own hand, which is the distinguishing mark in all my letters. This is how I write." This was a mark of authentication against the possibility of fraud, see 2:2.

Learning from numbers

318 The return of Jesus is mentioned 318 times in the New Testament, which is more than any other doctrine. It is the theme of 2 Thessalonians chapters 1 and 2.

OUTLINE		
1. Jesus will come again		1:1-12
2. Events before Jesus' coming		2:1-17
3. How to live in the light of Jesus' coming		3:1-18

1 Timothy

KEYS TO UNLOCK 1 TIMOTHY	
KEY VERSE	*"Fight the good fight of the faith. Take hold of the eternal life to which you were called when you made your good confession in the presence of many witnesses"* 6:12.
KEY WORD	*Trustworthy*
KEY PHRASE	*Teach these things*
KEY PASSAGE	*Chapter 1, where false teaching and legalism are condemned*
KEY THOUGHT	*A manual giving the qualifications for leadership in the church.*

Names and titles of God in 1 Timothy

- Our Savior 1:1
- Blessed God 1:11
- King 1:17
- One God 2:5
- The living God 3:15

Name of letter

Pros Timotheon A, the "First to Timothy," is the Greek title for this letter. Timothy means "honored by God," or "honoring God," and the name was most probably given to him by his God-fearing mother Eunice, 2 Timothy 1:5.

Author

The Pauline authorship of the Pastoral Letters (1 Timothy, 2 Timothy and Titus) has been questioned more than any of his other letters. A general point about this is that it is quite true that these letters have a different style and language from the rest of his letters.

For example, in the three Pastoral Letters there are 82 words in 1 Timothy, 53 words in 2 Timothy, and 33 words in Titus, which are not found in any of Paul's other ten New Testament letters. However, they were written later and about different topics than his other letters. So this could be the simple explanation for using a different vocabulary.

Date

AD 63–65.

Theme and purpose

While this is a personal letter it contains much that is relevant to any Christian, especially to ministers and all church workers.

- It warns against false teaching in the church.
- It has instructions about church administration and worship.
- It states the kind of people who should be church leaders.

OUTLINE		
1.	Introduction and charge to Timothy	1:1-20
2.	Instructions for the church and its officers	1:21–3:16
3.	The need for spiritual discernment	4:1-16
4.	Practical instructions	5:1-25
5.	Godliness and riches	6:1-21

2 Timothy

KEYS TO UNLOCK 2 TIMOTHY	
KEY VERSE	*"Endure hardship with us like a good soldier of Christ Jesus"* 2:4.
KEY WORD	*Endure*
KEY PHRASE	*Be strong*
KEY PASSAGE	*Chapter 2, as it describes the keys for faithful Christian ministry*
KEY THOUGHT	*I have finished the race.*

Names and titles of Jesus in 2 Timothy

- Christ Jesus 1:1
- Lord 1:2
- Savior 1:10

Name of letter

The title given to this letter, the last one we have of Paul's, was *Pros Timotheon B*, the "Second to Timothy." As Paul's letters were collected together the letter *B* would have been added to this one to distinguish it from 1 Timothy.

Author

See *1 Timothy, Author.*

Date

AD 62–63.

Setting

Paul's second imprisonment in Rome was quite different from his house arrest which is mentioned at the end of Acts 28. Paul was now chained up like a common criminal, 1:16; 29, in a freezing dungeon, 4:13.

Paul knew that his own execution could take place at any time, 4:6-8.

Theme and purpose

Paul gave Timothy short, sharp instructions to follow: 1:6; 1:8, 12-13; 1:13; 1:14; 2:1; 2:3; 2:15; 2:22; 2:23; and 4:15, "Be on your guard against him [Alexander the metal worker.]"

Special features of 2 Timothy

This letter, effectively Paul's last will and testament, shows how much Paul missed human companionship and Christian fellowship.

- Paul had been deserted by Demas, 4:10 and by "everyone in the province of Asia," 1:15.
- Only faithful Dr Luke was with Paul, 4:11.
- Paul twice asked Timothy to visit him in prison "Do your best to come to me quickly" 4:9. "Do your best to get have before winter" 4:21. For Paul longed to see Timothy again, 1:4, as he was his spiritual son, Philippians 2:22, "as a son with a father he has served with me."

OUTLINE		
1.	A father's counsel	1:1-18
2.	Christian workers take note	2:1-26
3.	Paul's last days	3:1-17
4.	Paul's last words	4:1-22

The Pastoral Letters

1 Timothy, 2 Timothy, Titus

The three letters, 1 Timothy, 2 Timothy and Titus, are known as the Pastoral Letters. In these letters the focus of attention is on caring for God's flock. These letters became known as "The Pastoral Letters" in the eighteenth century, but had been referred to as such much earlier. For example Aquinas, in 1274, wrote of 1 Timothy, "This letter is, as it were, a pastoral rule which the apostle Paul delivered to Timothy."

These letters were most probably written shortly after Paul's house arrest in Rome, Acts 28, in about AD 60–62.

A fourth missionary journey?

After Paul was released from his arrest it is likely that he set out on his fourth missionary journey. From Acts 13:1–21:17 it is clear that Paul went on three missionary tours. Evidence that Paul did go on a fourth missionary tour is based on information gleaned from:

- Romans 15:24, 28, where Paul states his desire to visit Spain.
- Eusebius, the renowned historian, who implies that Paul was indeed released from his first imprisonment in Rome, *Ecclesiastical History*, 2.22.2-3.
- Clement of Rome, who in his Epistle to the Corinthians, chapter 5, states that Paul preached the gospel in Spain.

Paul's actions

During this fourth missionary tour, Paul:

- placed Titus as the leading pastor in Crete;
- left Timothy to care for the church at Ephesus;
- moved on himself to Philippi, where he wrote 1 Timothy and his letter to Titus, in about AD 63–65;
- went back to Rome where he was imprisoned again, and where he wrote 2 Timothy, while he expected imminent execution, around AD 67–68.

Themes in the Pastoral Letters

1. *"A trustworthy saying,"* This phrase is unique to the Pastoral Letters, where it is used five times. Paul used it to refer to Christian sayings and traditions, and to identify key sayings. See 1 Timothy 1:15; 3:1; 4:9 2 Timothy 2:11; Titus 3:8.
2. *Godliness*, 1 Timothy 2:2.
3. *Controversies*, 1 Timothy 1:4; 6:4; 2 Timothy 2:23; Titus 3:9.

Titus

KEYS TO UNLOCK TITUS	
KEY VERSE	*"He saved us, not because of righteous things we had done, but because of his mercy. He saved us through the washing of rebirth and renewal by the Holy Spirit" 3:5.*
KEY WORD	*Teach*
KEY PHRASE	*Sound doctrine*
KEY PASSAGE	*Chapter 2, with its instructions for conduct and doctrinal teaching*
KEY THOUGHT	*Christians should live godly lives.*

Names and titles of God in Titus

• Savior 1:3   • Father 1:4

Name of letter

This letter is just named *Pros Titon*, "To Titus." This name "Titus" was also the name of the Roman general who destroyed Jerusalem in AD 70 and then became the Roman Emperor.

Author

See *1 Timothy, Author.*

Date

AD 62–63.

Setting

While Titus is not mentioned at all in Acts there are 13 references to him in Paul's letters.

• Titus came to faith in Jesus through Paul, 1:4.

• Titus must have accompanied Paul on his third missionary journey as Paul sent him to Corinth three times during this time, 2 Corinthians 2:12, 13; 7:5-7, 13-15; 8:6, 16-24.
• Paul left Titus to carry on the work of leading the church there, 1:5.
• Paul regarded Titus as a reliable and gifted fellow-worker, 2 Corinthians 8:23, and brother, 2 Corinthians 3:13.

Theme and purpose

Paul wrote his letter to Titus:

1. To tell him what sort of church leaders should be appointed.
2. To tell him how to teach the various groups in the church: the older men, the older women (who are to teach the younger women), the young men, and the slaves.
3. To tell Titus to remind the believers to be gentle and friendly, and to avoid hatred and divisions within the church.

Special features of Titus

The letter to Titus gives three excellent summaries of Christian theology:

• 1:1-4   • 1:11-14   • 3:4-7

OUTLINE	
1. Greetings, and qualities needed in an elder	1:1-16
2. Duties of five groups within the church	2:1-15
3. Keep on doing good, conclusion	3:1-15

Philemon

KEYS TO UNLOCK PHILEMON	
KEY VERSE	*"...no longer as a slave, but better than a slave, as a dear brother. He is very dear to me but even dearer to you, both as a man and as a brother in the Lord"* verse 16.
KEY WORD	*Useful*
KEY PHRASE	*In Christ*
KEY THOUGHT	*I appeal to you on the basis of love.*

Names and titles of Jesus in Philemon

- Lord Jesus Christ 5
- Lord Jesus 5
- Christ Jesus 6
- Christ 8
- Lord 20

Name of letter

Because of Philemon's name in verse 1 this letter became known as *Pros Philemona*, "To Philemon." Like the Pastoral Letters it is addressed to an individual, but unlike them it is also addressed to a church and to a family, verse 2.

Author

The apostle Paul, see verses 1, 9, 19, and Colossians 4:9-10, 12, 14; Philemon verses 10, 23-24.

Date

This letter, along with Paul's letter to the Colossians, was delivered by Tychicus and Onesimus, and so must have been written at the same time as Colossians, in about AD 60.

Setting

Philemon, a close friend of Paul's, owned a slave, Onesimus.

Onesimus had run away from his master, but had come into contact with Paul, and through him had become a follower of Jesus, verse 10, and see Colossians 4:9.

According to Roman law runaway slaves were liable to severe punishment, if they were not condemned to a violent death.

So Paul writes from prison in order to plead with Philemon to have Onesimus back. He uses all his powers of persuasion, and refers to himself as "an old man and now also a prisoner of Christ Jesus," verse 9.

Theme and purpose

Paul appeals to the highest of Christian principles when he writes, "welcome him [Onesimus] as you would welcome me," verse 17. Commenting on this verse Martin Luther wrote: "Even as Christ did for us with God the Father, thus Paul also does for Onesimus with Philemon."

OUTLINE		
1.	Introduction and Paul's praise of Philemon	1-7
2.	Paul's appeal for Onesimus, conclusion	8-25

Hebrews

KEYS TO UNLOCK HEBREWS	
KEY VERSE	*"Let us fix our eyes on Jesus, the author and perfecter of our faith, who for the joy set before him endured the cross, scorning its shame, and sat down at the right hand of the throne of God" 12:2.*
KEY WORD	*Superior*
KEY PHRASE	*Once for all*
KEY PASSAGE	*Chapter 11, rightly known as "The Hall of Fame of the Scriptures"*
KEY THOUGHT	*The author writes to show how Jesus fulfills the expectations of the Old Testament as he is God's final revelation to humankind.*

Names and titles of God in Hebrews

- Father 1:5
- Majesty in heaven 8:1
- The living God 9:14
- The Father of our spirits 12:9
- The judge of all men 12:23
- A consuming fire 12:29
- The God of peace 13:20 "May the God of peace... equip you with everything good for doing his will" 13:29.

Name of letter

The oldest title of this letter is *Pros Ebraious*, "To Hebrews." It is true that in the *King James Version* of the Bible the title given to this letter is: "The Epistle of Paul the Apostle to the Hebrews," but the earliest manuscripts give no support to this.

Author

It used to be thought that Paul wrote this letter, but today this view is not generally held as the writing style is so different from Paul's and since, unlike Paul, the writer never identifies himself in his letter. The short answer is that nobody knows who wrote the letter to the Hebrews, and so it is best to agree with Origen who said, "God alone knows the truth of the matter."

Date

Nobody knows for certain the year in which this letter was written. But there are three facts that probably narrow it down to between AD 65 and AD 69.

1. This letter was known to Clement of Rome, so it must have been written before AD 95.
2. If the persecution referred to in chapter 10 was the one instigated by Nero that would place the writing of this letter after AD 64.
3. The biggest clue about the date of writing of this letter is that the author refers to the temple and the priestly activities linked to it in the present tense, 5:1-3; 7:23, 27; 8:3-5; 9:6-9, 13, 25; 10:1, 3, 4, 8, 11; 13:10, 11. It seems inconceivable that the author would not have referred to the destruction of the temple in Jerusalem, which took place in AD 70, if the temple was no longer standing.

Setting

From the contents of the letter itself it is possible to build up quite a comprehensive picture of the recipients of this letter, even if we may never know who wrote it, or from where it was written.

- The recipients were believers, 3:1.
- The recipients had become believers through the testimony of eyewitnesses of Jesus, 2:3.
- The recipients had endured hardship because of the stand they had taken for the gospel, 10:32-34.
- The recipients had become slow to learn, 5:11.
- The recipients were in danger of drifting away, 2:1; 3:12.
- The recipients were especially susceptible to the impending persecution, 12:4-12.

Theme and purpose

The letter to the Hebrews presents Jesus as

- the divine-human Prophet
- Priest
- King.

His deity and his humanity are equally stressed. Jesus is given a number of titles which describe his attributes, and emphasize how superior he is to all who were before him.

1. Jesus is the eternal Son of God, and so superior to all the Old Testament prophets, to the angels, and to Moses.
2. God declared Jesus to be the eternal priest, who is superior to all the priests of the Old Testament.
3. As High Priest Jesus gives true salvation, which all the rituals and animals sacrifices of the Old Testament could only foreshadow:

Sacrifices under the Law: 10:1-4

- Reminders of sin
- Repeated constantly

- Anticipation
- Shadows
- Blood of animals
- Involuntary

The sacrifice of Jesus, 10:5-18

- Remover of sin
- Once for all time
- Fulfillment
- Substance
- Blood of Jesus
- Voluntary

Special features of Hebrews

There are a number of things about the letter to the Hebrews which are different from other New Testament letters.

1. The opening of the letter does not state who it is written by or who it is written to. This is unique among the New Testament letters.
2. This letter acts as a commentary and interpretation of the book of Leviticus, as it shows the superiority of Christianity over Judaism.
3. This letter has been called "The Faith" book, as no other New Testament letter has so much to say on this subject.
4. Hebrews has severe warnings about drifting away from God, 2:1; 3:12, 13; 4:1, 11; 12:1-3, 13, 15.
5. The letter to the Hebrews is full of quotations to and allusions from the Old Testament. However, it is sometimes difficult to tell when the Old Testament is being quoted

and when the writer is summarizing a thought from the Old Testament, as there are no phrases in this letter like, "It is written," or "This happened that the scripture might be fulfilled which said," as are found in the Gospels.

Learning from numbers

13 The word "better" comes 13 times in this letter. The "better" things in the letter to the Hebrews:

1. Better revelation, 1:1-4
2. Better things, 6:9
3. Better covenant, 7:22
4. Better priesthood, 7:23-28
5. Better sacrifice, 9:23
6. Better possessions, 10:34
7. Better country [a heavenly one], 11:16
8. Better resurrection, 11:35

15 The word "heaven," or "heavenly" is used 15 times in this letter.

OUTLINE		
1.	The Son is superior to angels	1:1–2:18
2.	The Son is superior to Moses	3:1-19
3.	The Son is superior to Joshua	4:1-13
4.	The Son is a superior High Priest	4:14–10:39
5.	Faith and the Christian life	11:1–13:17
6.	Conclusion	13:18-25

James

KEYS TO UNLOCK JAMES	
KEY VERSE	*"As the body without the spirit is dead, so faith without deeds is dead"* 2:26.
KEY WORD	*Deeds*
KEY PHRASE	*Mercy triumphs over judgment*
KEY PASSAGE	*Chapter 1, with its teaching on trials and temptations*
KEY THOUGHT	*James gives a wide variety of instructions to guide Christians in their belief and behavior.*

Names and titles of God in James

- The Father of the heavenly lights 1:17
- Father 1:27
- Lord 4:10
- Lord Almighty 5:4

Name of letter

The early title for this letter is *Jakobou Epistole*, "Epistle of James." It is based on the name *Jakobos*, (James in 1:1). *Jacobos* is the Greek form of the Hebrew name Jacob which was a common Jewish name in the first century.

Author

The author of this letter, 1:1, is called "James," but there are four men in the New Testament who are called by this name. However, James the father of Judas (not Iscariot), and James, the son of Alphaeus, one of the 12 apostles about whom we know nothing, are highly unlikely to have been the author of this letter as they were hardly authoritative figures for such a task. A third James, the son of Zebedee and brother of John might have been a good candidate if he had not been martyred, Acts 12:2, in AD 44, a date much too early for the writing of this letter.

This leaves a fourth James, who was one of Jesus' half-brothers, "'Isn't this the carpenter's son? Isn't his mother's name Mary, and aren't his brothers James, Joseph, Simon and Judas?'" *Matthew 13:55*

Date

The letter must have been written before AD 62 when James was martyred and may well have been written as early as AD 50 which would make it one of the earliest New Testament letters.

Setting

The New Testament has the following information about James:

- He may have been the eldest half-brother to Jesus since he is named first in Matthew 13:55.
- He is singled out as being one of the people whom Jesus appeared to after his resurrection, 1 Corinthians 15:7.
- In Galatians 2:9 Paul refers to him as a "pillar" of the church.
- When Paul made his first visit to Jerusalem after his conversion he met James, Galatians 1:9.
- After Peter was miraculously

delivered from prison he told his friends to let James know about this, Acts 12:17.

- The council of Jerusalem was headed up by James, Acts 15:13.

Theme and purpose
1. The fatherhood of God
James teaches that:

a. God answers prayer generously, 1:5.
b. God promises life to persecuted Christians, 1:12.
c. God never tempts, 1:13.
d. God never changes his attitude towards believers, 1:16-18.
e. God chooses the poor, 2:5.
f. God makes humankind in his likeness, 3:9.
g. God opposes the proud, 4:6.

h. God's grace is always available when we need it, 4:6, 8.

2. Hating sin

a. Sin originates in humankind's nature, 1:14; 3:6, 16: 4:1-3, 5.
b. Sin may have a small beginning but it quickly spreads, 1:15; 3:5.
c. Sin is defined as offending God and meriting his judgment, 2:10-13; 4:12; 5:1.
d. The Lord's grace can forgive sin, 2:13; 4:6; 5:11, 20.

3. Christian character and behavior must become mature

a. God develops Christian character through:
  - trials and suffering, 1:2-4
  - the Word of God, 1:21
  - practical obedience, 1:22-25
  - drawing near to God, 4:8
  - humility, 4:10.
b. Descriptions of Christian character are given in 3:13-18; 4:13-17; 5:7-11.
c. Christian behavior is outlined in 1:26, 27; 2:1-26; 3:1-12; 4:11, 12; 5:12-20.

OUTLINE		
1.	Genuine spirituality	1:1-27
2.	Faith and deeds	2:1-26
3.	Curbing the tongue	3:1-18
4.	Practical exhortations	4:1–5:7
5.	Prayer and patience	5:8-20

1 Peter

KEYS TO UNLOCK 1 PETER	
KEY VERSE	*"Dear friends, do not be surprised at the painful trial you are suffering, as though something strange were happening to you" 4:12.*
KEY WORD	*Suffering*
KEY PHRASE	*Prepare your minds for action*
KEY PASSAGE	*Chapter 1, with its promises for believers*
KEY THOUGHT	*Peter wrote this letter to encourage Christians who were being persecuted.*

Names and titles of God in 1 Peter

- Father 1:2
- Lord 1:25
- God of all grace 5:10

Name of letter

The early title of this letter was *Petrou A*, "First of Peter," which was derived from its opening words: *Petros apostolos Iesou Christou*, "Peter, an apostle of Jesus Christ."

Author

The letter itself states that Peter was its author, and this is confirmed in the letter which reflects incidents in Peter's life and his distinctive character, 1:12; 4:13; 5:1, 2, 13.

Date

The apostle Peter states that he was writing from "Babylon," 5:13, a code-name for Rome. Peter probably wrote this letter in AD 64 as Nero's persecution of Christians was starting. In about AD 67/68 Peter himself was martyred in Rome.

Special features of 1 Peter

In his letter Peter keeps coming back to particular words which reflect what is on his mind.

1. Hope, 1:3, 13, 21; 3:15
2. Grace and mercy, 1:2, 3, 10, 13; 2:10; 3:7, 4:10; 5:5, 10, 12
3. Love, 1:8, 22; 2:17; 3:8, 10; 4:8; 5:14
4. Salvation, 1:5, 9, 10; 2:2
5. Being sober, 1:13; 4:7; 5:8
6. Joy, 1:6, 8; 4:13
7. Humility, 3:8; 5:5, 6
8. Fear, 1:17; 2:16, 17; 3:14
9. Glory, 1:7, 11, 21, 24; 4:11, 13, 14; 5:1, 4, 10
10. Precious, 1:7, 19; 2:4, 6, 7; 3:4.

OUTLINE		
1.	Greeting and Christian salvation	1:1–2:10
2.	Christian relationships	2:11–3:12
3.	Christian suffering	3:13–4:19
4.	Christian community	5:1-14

2 Peter

KEYS TO UNLOCK 2 PETER	
KEY VERSE	*"I want you to recall the words spoken in the past by the holy prophets and the command given by our Lord and Savior through your apostles" 3:2.*
KEY WORD	*Knowledge*
KEY PHRASE	*False teachers*
KEY PASSAGE	*Chapter 2, with its warning against false teachers*
KEY THOUGHT	*Peter warns his readers that they are in danger of lapsing into immorality if they listen to false teaching.*

Names and titles of God in 2 Peter

- Father 1:17
- Lord 2:11

Name of letter

To distinguish this letter from 1 Peter it was given the Greek title *Petrou B,* "Second Peter."

Author

The opening verse of this letter states who wrote it: "Simon Peter, a servant and apostle of Jesus Christ." The writer also claims to have been an eyewitness of Jesus' ascension, 1:16-18, see Matthew 17:15, and we know that only Peter, James and John were present at this event. The writer also mentions that this is his second letter, 3:1, and he refers to Paul as "our dear brother," 3:15. There are convincing reasons from within the letter itself to conclude that it was written by the apostle Peter.

Date

As 2 Peter was written after 1 Peter, and since it was written towards the end of Peter's life, see 1:12-15, and since Peter was martyred in AD 67/68, this letter was probably written around AD 65–68.

Setting

This letter contrasts the knowledge and practice of truth with that of the false teachers. These false teachers seem to have claimed that they had special knowledge which they said meant that they could dispense with certain Christian teaching. For example they were encouraging sexual excesses and they did this in the name of Jesus, 2:13. "With eyes full of adultery, they never stop sinning," 2:14. Peter's warning is summed up in 3:17, "Do not be carried away by the error of lawless men and fall from your secure position."

Another heresy Peter attacks concerned Jesus' return, which was being questioned by the false teachers. Peter's reply to this is that a thousand years is like a day, and a day is like a thousand years with the Lord, 3:8.

OUTLINE		
1.	Living a Christian life	Chapter 1
2.	Ungodliness	Chapter 2
3.	Jesus will return	Chapter 3

1 John

KEYS TO UNLOCK 1 JOHN	
KEY VERSE	*"I write this to you who believe in the name of the Son of God so that you may know that you have eternal life" 5:13.*
KEY WORD	*Fellowship*
KEY PHRASE	*Dear friends/dear children*
KEY PASSAGE	*Chapter 5, with its teaching about Christian assurance*
KEY THOUGHT	*If we claim to love God we must show this by loving one another.*

Names and titles of God in 1 John

- Father 1:2 • Light 1:5 • Love 4:8

Name of letter

The original title given to this book was *Ioannou A*, "1 John," even though the name "John" does not appear anywhere in the book.

Author

Most New Testament letters state who the author is, but this is not the case with 1 John. However, in addition to early church fathers from the second century, such as Irenaeus, Clement of Alexandria and Tertullian, who stated that this letter was written by the apostle John, there are a number of indications that this was indeed the case which can be found in the letter itself.

- Eyewitnesses to Jesus' life are mentioned, 1:1-4.
- There are many striking similarities between John's Gospel and 1 John, especially in the use of contrasts between love and hate, darkness and light, and life and death.
- The writer of 1 John clearly knew about having a very close relationship with Jesus, 1:1; 2:5, 6, 24, 27, 28, which fits with the description of "the disciple whom Jesus loved" reclining "next to him" at the Lord's Supper, John 13:23.

Date

It is not possible to date the writing of 1 John precisely. But as it was probably written after John's Gospel, when John was quite elderly, a date between AD 85 and 95 is probable.

Theme and purpose

John wrote to warn his readers against the false teachers. If they heeded their teaching their fellowship with God the Father and Jesus would be in danger of being upset. The false teachers claimed that Jesus could not really have been a human being, so John emphasizes the reality of Jesus' humanity, 1:1-4.

OUTLINE	
1. Introduction	1:1-4
2. Light and darkness	1:5–2:29
3. Dealing with sinfulness	3:1-24
4. Living in love	4:1-21
5. Fellowship	5:1-21

2 John and 3 John

KEYS TO UNLOCK 2 JOHN & 3 JOHN	
KEY VERSE IN 2 JOHN	*"And this is love: that we walk in obedience to his commands. As you have heard from the beginning, his command is that you walk in love" 2 John 6.*
KEY VERSE IN 3 JOHN	*"I have no greater joy than to hear that my children are walking in the truth" 3 John 4.*
KEY WORD IN 2 JOHN	*Love*
KEY WORD IN 3 JOHN	*Truth*
KEY THOUGHT IN 2 JOHN	*In the face of the false teachers, keep on loving one another.*
KEY THOUGHT IN 3 JOHN	*Gaius is singled out for praise for helping fellow Christians.*

Names and titles of Jesus in 2 and 3 John

- Lord Jesus Christ 2 John 3
- Son of the Father 2 John 3
- Jesus Christ 2 John 7
- The Son 2 John 9
- Christ 2 John 9
- The Name 3 John 7

Name of letter

The early Greek titles for these letters were *Ioannou B*, "Second of John," and *Ioannou C*, "Third of John."

Author

The "elder" of 2 John verse 1, and 3 John verse 1, has traditionally been identified as being John the apostle.

Date

The probable dates for these two letters are AD 85 to AD 95.

Setting

In the first two centuries Christians were used to welcoming traveling Christian evangelists into their homes. John wrote 2 John to warn Christians to be discerning about this and not to allow any false teachers to enjoy their welcome and hospitality, see also 3 John verse 5.

In 3 John the writer warns against the malicious teaching of Diotrephes and encourages Gaius to show hospitality to genuine Christian travelers.

OUTLINE	
2 John	
1. Greeting, and love one another	verses 1-6
2. Beware of false teachers, greetings	7-13
3 John	
1. Greeting, and supporting God's servants	1-8
2. Beware of Diotrephes	9-10
3. Well done Demetrius, conclusion	11-15

Jude

KEYS TO UNLOCK JUDE	
KEY VERSE	*"To him who is able to keep you from falling and to present you before his glorious presence without fault and with great joy…"* verse 24.
KEY WORD	*Keep*
KEY PHRASE	*Contend for the faith*
KEY PASSAGE	
KEY THOUGHT	*Jude warns against the perverse teaching of the false teachers.*

Names and titles of God in

- Father 1
- Lord God 4
- The Lord 5

Name of letter

The original Greek title given to this letter was *Iouda*, "Of Jude." This name can be translated as either "Jude" or "Judas" and was a popular name in the first century.

Author

The opening verse of the letter identifies the author as "Jude," and as "a servant of Jesus Christ and a brother of James." This was like saying "the brother of the well-known James," which would be referring to the James who was a half-brother of Jesus. This would also make the author of this letter, Jude, a half-brother of Jesus. "'Isn't his mother's name Mary, and aren't his brothers James, Joseph, Simon and Judas?'" *Matthew 13:55*

Date

There are obvious similarities between 2 Peter and Jude, see 2 Peter chapter 2 and Jude 4-18. Some have concluded that Jude may have had 2 Peter in mind as he wrote, or that Peter had Jude's letter in mind as he wrote his second letter. In ancient writing it was not uncommon to make use of other people's writing. If Jude used 2 Peter then Jude may have been written as late as AD 80, but if Peter used Jude, Jude may have been written as early as AD 65.

Theme and purpose

Jude reminds the believers that they have to take responsibility for the gospel which includes defending it.

OUTLINE		
1.	Greetings and reason for letter	1-4
2.	Warning against false teachers	5-16
3.	Exhortations to Christians	17-23
4.	Blessing	24-25

Revelation

KEYS TO UNLOCK REVELATION	
KEY VERSE	*"Write, therefore, what you have seen, what is now and what will take place later"* 1:19.
KEY WORD	*Overcomes*
KEY PHRASE	*They follow the Lamb*
KEY PASSAGE	*Chapter 19, and Jesus' coming glory*
KEY THOUGHT	*The book of Revelation is the revelation of Jesus Christ, 1:1.*

Names and titles of God in Revelation

- Father 1:6
- Lord God Almighty 4:8
- Living God 7:2
- God of heaven 11:13
- Lord 11:15
- King of the Ages 15:3

Name of letter

The original Greek title of this book is *Apokalypsis Ioannou*, "Revelation of John."

This book is also known as the Apocalypse, a word which is a transliteration of the Greek word *apokalypsis*, meaning "unveiling," "disclosure," or "revelation." The book unveils truths which would otherwise remain hidden.

The book should not be called the book of "Revelations" in the plural, as that is not its name, and because that rather goes counter to the unity of the book.

Perhaps the best name for the book comes in the opening verse, "The revelation of Jesus Christ." This could mean either a revelation that came from Jesus, or a revelation about Jesus Christ. Both would be appropriate.

Author

The early church fathers, including Justin Martyr, Clement of Alexandria, Irenaeus and the church historian Eusebius all believed that this book was written by the apostle John while he was in exile on the Mediterranean island of Patmos, 1:9.

The book itself, four times, mentions that its author is John, 1:1, 4, 9; 22:8. This view has been contested from as early as the third century. Among many objections to John being the author of this book, the following three have been put forward:

1. The Greek writing in the book of Revelation is rather unusual, and not at all similar to the Greek in John's Gospel.
2. In John's Gospel John never mentions himself by name, but does so four times in the book of Revelation.
3. The themes of love and truth, which are the characteristic themes of John's Gospel are almost absent in the book of Revelation.

These objections to John being the author of Revelation have been countered in the following ways:

1. The Greek in Revelation is not bad Greek, but is deliberately unusual

because it deals with unusual topics and so suits the subject matter.

2. In John's Gospel John may have thought it best to keep his name out of the book as the whole purpose of it was to point to Jesus. However, in the book of Revelation he may have mentioned his own name to show that this revelation really did come to a person, and he was that person.

3. As the book of Revelation has judgment as its central theme we should not be too surprised if it does not cover the same ground as John's Gospel.

There is plenty of evidence to support the traditional view that the apostle John wrote five New Testament books: his Gospel, three letters and the book of Revelation.

Date

It is not possible to be sure about the exact date at which this letter was written. One of the determining factors hinges on which persecution of Christians is being referred to in John's writing. If Nero's persecutions are being described that would place the writing of the book around AD 54–68; but if the persecutions refer to those under Domitian, then the date would be much later, around AD 81–96.

Setting

For many people, the book of Revelation

is the most difficult book in the New Testament to understand. That is because it comes in the *genre* of apocalyptic, and most people today are not familiar with this type of literature in general, let alone with the seemingly impossible to understand symbols and other details in the book of Revelation.

The problem is further aggravated because Christians have different ways of interpreting this book. The four main interpretations are as follows:

1. The preterist way of interpretation

The Latin word *praeter* means "past." This view does not think that the book is a prophecy about the future. It thinks that it describes past events, events that are restricted to the first century. This view interprets all the symbolism in the book as pointers to the Roman persecution of the church, to emperor worship, and to the divine judgment of Rome. This view holds that most of the descriptions in Revelation have already taken place. The preterist view is sometimes called the "historic" view, but should not be muddled up with the "historicist" view which now follows!

2. The historicist way of interpretation
This way of interpreting the book of Revelation believes that it is an allegorical panorama of the history of the Christian church from the first century until Jesus comes again. This view thinks that there are snapshots of the history of the church throughout the book of Revelation.

3. The symbolic or idealist way of interpretation
This view rules out the idea that the book of Revelation is anything to do with predictive prophecy. It views the book as a symbolic portrait of the cosmic conflict. This view does not attempt to interpret the most mysterious visions but it simply stresses the spiritual principles that run through the book. For this reason this view has been called the "spiritualizing" view. This view sees the book as a description of the general struggle between the Christian church and evil, which has been going

on for the past 2,000 years, and in which good defeats evil.

4. The futurist way of interpretation
The futurist view believes that the book of Revelation contains a forecast of universal history. This view believes that the focus of the book of Revelation is primarily on the end times. This view interprets 1:19 to mean that most of the book is about the future and this view discounts all historical allusions.

It is not necessary to rigidly adopt any one way of interpreting Revelation. Prophecies often have two points of reference: an event close to hand and an event in the distant future. For example Isaiah's prophecy about a child (Isaiah 7:14) refers both to a young woman in Isaiah's day and to Mary, the mother of Jesus. In the same way, the prophecies in the book of Revelation can be taken to refer to two events: to the events in the time of persecution under the Roman Emperor Domitian, and to the events which will usher in the end of time.

OUTLINE	
1. The seven letters to the seven churches	1:1–3:22
2. World events before Jesus' return	4:1–19:21
3. The last judgment	20:1-15
4. The new heaven and the new earth	21:1–22:21

6 STUDYING BIBLE PEOPLE

Introduction

What's in a name? In Bible times names were more significant and were more revealing than they are today. This chapter starts with examples of the importance of names.

Unlike today's historians, biblical writers did not attempt to give complete pictures of the people about whom they were writing. They were highly selective in their choice of material, including only those facts which fitted in with their overall aims and emphases — emphases which were quite different from those of secular writers.

We have, for example, no idea what Jesus looked like, and with one exception (his visit to Jerusalem as a 12-year-old) none of the Gospels tell us anything about Jesus' life from the time he went to Nazareth as a toddler until he was about 30 years old.

Mark devotes over a third of his Gospel — six out of 16 chapters — to the last week of Jesus' life and his death and resurrection. From this we can clearly see what was of overriding importance to Mark.

The record of God's interaction with the men and women in the Bible is a great encouragement to us today. We learn both from their failings and from their faithfulness to God.

What do the names of Bible people mean?

Names and characters

In Bible times names were much more than mere labels. Hebrew names always meant something and it became an important part of the infant's life. Jewish people believed that if they knew the meaning of a person's name they would know the person himself.

Jacob

Jacob means "heel grabber." In his case it was obvious that to know his name was to know his character.

Abigail

Abigail said of her husband, "He is just like his name – his name is Fool, and folly goes with him" 1 Samuel 25:25.

Barnabas

Barnabas was given his distinctive name by the apostles, "son of encouragement," or "comforter," because they appreciated his compassionate nature.

After the exile

After the exile the meaning of names was less important. A person might be called "Daniel" not because of its meaning, "God is my judge," but to honor the famous person who was put in the lions' den.

There were exceptions to this. For example, the name "Jesus" is a Greek form of the Hebrew name "Joshua," meaning, "salvation of Yahweh."

Compound names

Many names were made up of more than one name which were then combined. Such names made little statements about the people who bore the name.

Immanuel

Immanuel, the name given to the coming Messiah, Isaiah 7:14, "God with us," underlines the fact that the Messiah will have a divine nature.

Theophoric names

Some compound names were theophoric names, having a divine name linked to a noun or verb, which when translated gave a short sentence for the name. A fragment of the divine name, such as "Ya" or "Ja" was added at the beginning or end of the name as the first or last syllables.

Jonathan

Jonathan means "The Lord has given."

Elijah

Elijah refers to the prophet's loyalty, meaning, "My God [is] the Lord."

This way of making compound names also applied to heathen names.

Meribbaal

In the case of "Meribbaal," Saul's grandson, 1 Chronicles 8:34, the word "Baal" has been added.

Names and circumstances

The choice of a child's name was sometimes derived from the

circumstances surrounding its birth.

Barak
A baby born during a rainstorm, such as Deborah's general, might be given the name "Barak," meaning lightning.

Ichabod
After the Philistines had captured the ark of the covenant from Israel, the mother who was giving birth to a baby called her baby "Ichabod" for the glory [chabod] had departed from Israel, 1 Samuel 4:21.

Names and animals
Animal names were sometimes given to children.

- **Rachel** means "sheep."
- **Deborah** means "bee."
- **Caleb** means "dog."

The firstborn son
It is common today for a firstborn son to be given the name of his father, but this did not happen in Bible times. For example, from Boaz to the last king of Judah, there are 24 kings, none of whom took the name of their father.

Hometowns and names
People who had the same name were sometimes distinguished by being given the name of their hometown. David's father was called "Jesse the Bethlehemite," 1 Samuel 16:1; the giant David killed was called "Goliath of Gath," 1 Samuel 17:4; Mary Magalene was known as "Mary of Magdala," Matthew 28:1.

Changing names
When a person became an adult his name was sometimes changed.

Mara
Naomi, Ruth's mother-in-law, wanted her name changed to "Mara" because she felt that the Lord had dealt very bitterly [mara] with her, Ruth 1:20.

Saul to Paul
Some time after Saul's conversion on the Damascus road he changed his name to Paul, Acts 13:1-13.

Jacob to Israel
An angel gave Jacob his new name of Israel, Genesis 32:26.

Simon to Peter
Jesus gave Simon the new name of Peter, Matthew 16:17, 18.

In the name of
In Bible times the name was thought to be part of or an expression of the person himself. Speaking "in the name of" a person meant that you were speaking his thoughts or speaking in his authority. So when Jesus told his disciples to pray in his name, John 14:13, 14; 15:16; 16:23, 24, 26, he was telling them to identify themselves completely with him so that their prayers would be in complete harmony with his will.

Names of the Trinity: God the Father

Names and revelation

One of the main ways in which God teaches people about himself is through his name. All of the names of God found in the Bible express something important about God's nature.

Yahweh

The personal name of God in the Old Testament is Yahweh or Jehovah. It means "the One who is always present." In this way God pledged his presence would always be with his faithful followers.

NAMES OF GOD		
Original name	*English translation*	*Meaning*
HEBREW		
El Elyon	Most High	God, the maker of the universe, is sovereign. *Genesis 14:18-20*
Shapat	Judge	Because God is righteous he is the moral authority in the world. *Genesis 18:25*
El Olam	The eternal God	God has no beginning or end. *Genesis 21:33*
Yahweh-jireh	The Lord provides	God meets the needs of believers. *Genesis 22:14*
El Elohe-Yisra'el	God, the God of Israel	God gives a new name to his people. *Genesis 33:30*
El Shaddai	God of the mountains	God is all-powerful, *Genesis 49:25*
Yahweh-nissi	The Lord my banner	God gives victory. *Exodus 17:15*
Yahweh-shalom	The Lord is peace	God brings inner peace and makes us whole. *Judges 6:24*
El Berit	God of the covenant	God keeps his covenant. *Judges 9:46*
Yahweh-seba'ot	God of armies	God fights for his people and is all-powerful. *1 Samuel 17:45*
Adonai	Lord, Master	God has total authority. *Psalm 2:4*
Qedosh Yisra'el	Israel's holy One	God is holy. *Isaiah 1:4*
Yahweh-tsidkenu	The Lord our righteousness	God is righteous. *Jeremiah 23:6*
Yahweh-shammah	The Lord is there	God will always be with his people. *Ezekiel 48:35*
ARAMAIC		
Attiq yomin	Ancient of Days	God judges the world. *Daniel 7:9*
Illaya	Most High	God has the ultimate authority. *Daniel 7:18*
GREEK		
Theos ho Pater	God the Father	God is over all and loves the members of his family. *Ephesians 3:14*

Names of the Trinity: God the Son

Jesus

In the Gospels our Lord is called "Jesus," over 600 times, and 100 more times in the rest of the New Testament. It is the personal name that he was given at his birth, Matthew 1:21; Luke 1:31. Its basic meaning is "Savior," or "salvation."

Christ

This is the Greek word for the Hebrew "Messiah," meaning "anointed." This word comes some 50 times in the Gospels and over 200 times in the New Testament letters. "Christ" is an official title and is often written prefixed with the definite article: "The Christ."

When Jesus asked his disciples who they thought he was, Peter replied that he was "the Christ," the Son of the living God, Matthew 16:15, 16.

Jesus Christ

This double title only comes a few times in the Gospels but occurs frequently in the letters of Paul, Peter and John. The humble Man who was called "Jesus" on earth, is now exalted and glorified and is called "Christ." What he was as Jesus and what he is as Christ have combined and give the meaning of this title. The sufferings on earth and the glories of heaven are expressed in the title "Jesus Christ."

Lord Jesus Christ

This is the full written title of Jesus, and conveys his authority (Lord), his human nature (Jesus) and his glory (Christ.) In

this way his power and humanity and exultation are linked, Matthew 28:18.

Son of God

Jesus used this title to express his relationship to the Father, Matthew 11:27; Luke 10:22. God the Father addressed Jesus by this title at his baptism and transfiguration, Mark 1:11; 9:7. This title fully expresses who Jesus was.

Son of man

Jesus used this title of himself in the Gospels and it is not once used by another person to describe Jesus. By using this title Jesus was not merely referring to his humility in becoming a human being, but was laying claim to being the final representative of God to humankind.

Names of the Trinity: God the Holy Spirit

Old Testament and New Testament

In the Old Testament the third person of the Trinity is known as the Spirit, the Spirit of God, and the Spirit of the Lord.

In the New Testament he is known primarily as the Holy Spirit, but is also called the Spirit of Jesus, the Spirit of his [God's] Son, and the Spirit of Christ.

Ruah

In the Old Testament the Holy Spirit is called by the name *ruah* 378 times. *Ruah* has three basic meanings:

1. Wind

The Spirit is invisible, but it has powerful and mysterious ways of working: Genesis 8:1; Exodus 10:13, 19; Numbers 11:31; 1 Kings 18:45; Psalm 25:23; Jeremiah 10:13; Hosea 13:15; Jonah 4:8.

This Spirit is often linked to the idea of a violent and strong wind. "Then Moses stretched out his hand over the sea, and all that night the Lord drove the sea back with a strong east wind and turned it into dry land." *Exodus 14:21*

2. Breath or spirit

This mysterious force is seen as the life and vitality in a human being, Genesis 6:17; Psalm 31:5.

3. Divine power

This use of the word *ruah* describes moments when people appear to be carried outside themselves as a supernatural power overtakes them.

Early charismatic leaders experienced this, Judges 3:10, as did the early prophets, Numbers 24:2. "'The Spirit of the Lord will come upon you in power, and you will prophesy with them; and you will be changed into a different person,' Samuel promised Saul as he anointed him." *1 Samuel 10:6*

Pneuma

Pneuma is used 379 times in the New Testament to refer to the Holy Spirit.

Pneuma is used nearly 40 times to describe human beings having a spiritual relationship with God, Mark 2:8; Acts 7:59; Romans 1:9. "The Spirit himself testifies with our spirit that we are God's children." *Romans 8:16*

Pneuma is also used to describe a demonic spirit, Matthew 8:16; Mark 1:23, and on a few occasions to refer to heavenly spirits, Acts 23:8, 9.

But the most frequent use of *pneuma* in the New Testament, more than 250 times, is to refer to the Holy Spirit, that is, to the Spirit of God. For example, Jesus taught that the Holy Spirit would sustain his disciples during times of trial, Mark 13:11; John 14:15-17, 26; 15:26, 27; 16:7-15.

Abraham

Life of Abraham

- Son of Terah: Genesis 11:26, 27
- Marries Sarah: Genesis 11:29
- Lives in Ur, but moves to Haran: Genesis 11:31; Nehemiah 9:7; Acts 7:4
- And Canaan: Genesis 12:4, 5, 6; Acts 7:4
- God calls Abram: Genesis 12:1-3; Joshua 24:3; Nehemiah 9:7; Isaiah 51:2; Acts 7:2, 3; Hebrews 11:8
- Given Canaan: Genesis 12:1, 7; 15:7-21; Ezekiel 33:24
- Lives in Bethel: Genesis 12:8
- Goes to Egypt: Genesis 12:10-20; 26:1
- Deferring to Lot, chooses Hebron: Genesis 13; 14:13; 35:27
- Is blessed by Melchizedek: Genesis 14:18-20; Hebrews 7:1-10
- God's covenant with: Genesis 15; 17:1-22; Micah 7:20; Luke 1:73; Romans 4:13; 15:8; Hebrews 6:13, 14; Galatians 3:6-18, 29; 4:22-31
- Called "Abraham": Genesis 17:5; Nehemiah 9:7
- Circumcision of: Genesis 17:10-14, 23-27
- Angels appear to: Genesis 18:1-16; 22:11, 15; 24:7
- His questions about the destruction of the righteous and wicked in Sodom: Genesis 18:23-32
- Witnesses the destruction of Sodom: Genesis 19:27, 28
- Birth of Ishmael: Genesis 16:3, 15

- Lives in Gerar; deceives Abimelech about his wife Sarah: Genesis 20
- Birth of Isaac: Genesis 21:2, 3; Galatians 4:22-30
- Sends Hagar and Ishmael away: Genesis 21:10-14; Galatians 4:22-30
- Told to sacrifice Isaac: Genesis 22:1-19; Hebrews 11:17; James 2:21
- Sarah dies: Genesis 23:1, 2
- He buys a burial place for Sarah: Genesis 23:3-20
- Death: Genesis 15:15; 25:8-10

Character of Abraham

- Friend of God: Isaiah 41:8; 2 Chronicles 20:7; James 2:23
- Devotion of: Genesis 12:7, 8; 13:4, 18; 18:19; 20:7; 21:33; 22:3-13; 26:5; Nehemiah 9:7, 8; Romans 4:16-18; 2 Chronicles 20:7; Isaiah 41:8; James 2:23
- A prophet: Genesis 20:7
- Faith of: Genesis 15:6; Romans 4:1-22; Galatians 3:6-9; Hebrews 11:8-10, 17-19; James 2:21-24
- Unselfishness of: Genesis 13:9; 21:25-30
- Independence of: Genesis 14:23; 23:6-16
- Ancestors of, idolatrous: Joshua 24:2
- Assessment by his descendants: Matthew 3:9; Luke 13:16, 28; 19:9; John 8:33-40

Moses

Life of Moses

- A Levite and son of Amram: Exodus 2:1-4; 6:20; Acts 7:20; Hebrews 11:23
- Hidden in a small basket: Exodus 2:3
- Discovered and adopted by the daughter of Pharaoh: Exodus 2:5-10
- Learned in all the wisdom of Egypt: Acts 7:22
- His loyalty to his race: Hebrews 11:24-26
- Kills an Egyptian taskmaster; flees from Egypt; finds refuge among the Midianites: Exodus 2:11-22; Acts 7:24-29
- Links up with Jethro, priest of Midian; marries his daughter Zipporah; has one son, Gershom: Exodus 2:15-22
- Is a shepherd for Jethro in the desert of Horeb: Exodus 3:1
- Has the vision of the burning bush: Exodus 3:2-6
- God reveals to him his purpose to deliver the Israelites and bring them into the land of Canaan: Exodus 3:7-10
- Commissioned as leader of the Israelites: Exodus 3:10-22; 6:13
- His rod miraculously turned into a serpent, and his hand made leprous, and then restored: Exodus 4:1-9, 28
- With his wife and sons, he leaves Jethro for his work in Egypt: Exodus 4:18-20
- Meets Aaron in the wilderness: Exodus 4:27, 28
- With Aaron assembles the leaders of Israel: Exodus 4:29-31
- Along with Aaron, Moses goes before Pharaoh and demands, in God's name, that his people are set free: Exodus 5:1
- Rejected by Pharaoh; Israelites' suffering increased: Exodus 5
- People grumble about Moses and Aaron: Exodus 5:20, 21; 15:24; 16:2, 3; 17:2, 3; Numbers 14:2-4; 16:41; 20:2-5; 21:4-6; Deuteronomy 1:12, 26-28
- Receives comfort and assurance from the Lord: Exodus 6:1-8
- Unbelief of the people: Exodus 6:9
- Makes another appeal to Pharaoh: Exodus 6:11
- Under God's direction brings plagues on the land of Egypt: Exodus 7; 8; 9; 10; 11; 12
- Secures the deliverance of the people and leads them out of Egypt: Exodus 13
- Crosses the Red Sea; Pharaoh and his army are destroyed: Exodus 14
- Composes a song for the people of Israel to celebrate their deliverance from Pharaoh: Exodus 15
- Institutes a system of government: Exodus 18:13-26; Numbers 11:16-30; Deuteronomy 1:9-18
- Receives the law: Exodus 19; 20
- His face is transfigured: Exodus 34:29-35; 2 Corinthians 3:13
- Sets up the tabernacle: Exodus 26-31
- Reproves Aaron for making the golden calf: Exodus 32:22, 23

- Rebellion of Korah, Dathan and Abiram against Moses: Numbers 16
- Appoints Joshua as his successor: Numbers 27:22, 23; Deuteronomy 31:7, 8, 14, 23; 34:9
- Not permitted to enter Canaan, but views the land from the top of Mount Pisgah: Numbers 27:12-14; Deuteronomy 1:37; 3:23-29; 32:48-52; 34:1-8
- Death and burial of Moses: Numbers 31:2; Deuteronomy 32:50; 34:1-6
- Body of, disputed over: Jude 1:9
- 120 Years old at death: Deuteronomy 31:2
- Mourning for 30 days in the plains of Moab: Deuteronomy 34:8
- Present with Jesus on the Mount of Transfiguration: Matthew 17:3, 4; Mark 9:4; Luke 9:30
- A type of the Messiah: Deuteronomy 18:15-18; Acts 3:22; 7:37

Blessings of Moses

- Upon the people: Leviticus 9:23; Numbers 10:35, 36; Deuteronomy 1:11
- Last blessing on the 12 tribes: Deuteronomy 33

Character of Moses

- Grumbling of: Exodus 5:22, 23; Numbers 11:10-15
- Impatience of: Exodus 5:22, 23; 6:12; 32:19; Numbers 11:10-15; 16:15; 20:10; 31:14
- Respected and feared: Exodus 33:8

- Faith of: Numbers 10:29; Deuteronomy 9:1-3; Hebrews 11:23-28
- Called the man of God: Deuteronomy 33:1
- God spoke to Moses, as a man to his friend: Exodus 33:11
- Praised by God: Exodus 19:9; Numbers 14:12-20; Deuteronomy 9:13-29; with Exodus 32:30
- Magnanimity of, toward Eldad and Medad: Numbers 11:29
- Meekness of: Exodus 14:13, 14; 15:24, 25; 16:2, 3, 7, 8; Numbers 12:3; 16:4-11
- Obedience of: Exodus 7:6; 40:16, 19, 21

Prayers of Moses

- Numbers 14:12-20; Deuteronomy 9:13-29; with Exodus 32:30

Prophecies of Moses

- Exodus 3:10; 4:5, 11, 12; 6:13; 7:2; 17:16; 19:3-9; 33:11; Numbers 11:17; 12:7, 8; 36:13; Deuteronomy 1:3; 5:31; 18:15, 18; 34:10, 12; Hosea 12:13; Mark 7:9, 10; Acts 7:37, 38

David

David as king of Israel

- David's genealogy: Ruth 4:18-22; 1 Samuel 16:11; 17:12; 1 Chronicles 2:3-15; Matthew 1:1-6; Luke 3:31-38
- David as a shepherd: 1 Samuel 16:11
- Kills a lion and a bear: 1 Samuel 17:34-36
- Anointed king, while a youth, by the prophet Samuel, and inspired: 1 Samuel 16:1, 13; Psalm 89:19-37
- Chosen by God: Psalm 78:70
- Kills Goliath: 1 Samuel 17
- David's love for Jonathan: 1 Samuel 18:1-4
- Saul's jealousy of David: 1 Samuel 18:8-30
- Jonathan speaks up for David: 1 Samuel 19:1-7
- Writer of psalms: Psalm 17; 35; 52; 58; 64; 109; 142
- Conducts a campaign against, and defeats, the Philistines: 1 Samuel 19:8
- Saul attempts to kill him; he escapes to Ramah, and lives at Naioth, where Saul pursues him: 1 Samuel 19:9-24
- Jonathan makes covenant with him: 1 Samuel 20
- Escapes to Nob, where he eats consecrated bread and takes Goliath's sword from Abimelech: 1 Samuel 21:1-6; Matthew 12:3, 4
- Escapes to Gath: 1 Samuel 21:10-15
- Makes second covenant with

Jonathan: 1 Samuel 23:16-18
- Refrains from killing Saul: 1 Samuel 24
- Marries Nabal's widow, Abigail, and Ahinoam: 1 Samuel 25
- Lives in the wilderness of Ziph, has opportunity to kill Saul, but only takes his spear; Saul is contrite: 1 Samuel 26

- Death and burial of Saul and his
  sons: 1 Samuel 31;
  2 Samuel 21:1-14
- Kills the murderer of Saul:
  2 Samuel 1:1-16
- Lamentation over Saul:
  2 Samuel 1:17-27
- David goes to Hebron, and is
  anointed king over Judah:
  2 Samuel 2:1-4, 11; 5:5; 1 Kings
  2:11; 1 Chronicles 3:4; 11:1-3
- Anointed king of all Israel, and
  reigns 33 years: 2 Samuel 2:11; 5:5;
  1 Chronicles 3:4; 11:1-3; 12:23-40;
  29:27
- Captures Jerusalem: 2 Samuel 5:6;
  1 Chronicles 11:4-8; Isaiah 29:1
- Builds a palace: 2 Samuel 5:11;
  2 Chronicles 2:3
- Friendship with Hiram, king of Tyre:
  2 Samuel 5:11; 1 Kings 5:1
- Blessed by God: 2 Samuel 5:10;
  1 Chronicles 11:9
- David's fame: 1 Chronicles 14:17
- Philistines are defeated by David:
  2 Samuel 5:17, 25
- Assembles 30,000 men to escort the
  ark of the covenant to Jerusalem
  with music and thanksgiving:
  2 Samuel 6:1-5
- Uzzah is killed when he attempts to
  steady the ark of the covenant:
  2 Samuel 6:6-11
- David is terrified, and leaves the ark
  at the house of Obed-edom:
  2 Samuel 6:9-11
- After three months, David brings the
  ark of the covenant to Jerusalem

with dancing and great joy:
2 Samuel 6:12-16; 1 Chronicles 13
- Organized the tabernacle service:
  1 Chronicles 9:22; 15:16-24;
  16:4-6, 37-43
- Offers sacrifice, distributes gifts,
  and blesses the people:
  2 Samuel 6:17-19
- Michal rebukes him for his religious
  enthusiasm: 2 Samuel 6:20-23
- Desires to build a temple, is
  forbidden, but receives God's
  promise that his descendants will
  reign forever: 2 Samuel 7:12-16;
  23:5; 1 Chronicles 17:11-14; 2
  Chronicles 6:16; Psalm 89:3, 4;
  132:11, 12; Acts 15:16;
  Romans 15:12
- Interpretation and fulfillment of this
  prophecy: Acts 13:22, 23
- Shows Mephibosheth, the lame son
  of Saul, great kindness:
  2 Samuel 9:6; 19:24-30
- Commits adultery with Bathsheba:
  2 Samuel 11:2-5
- Instigates Uriah's death:
  2 Samuel 11:6-25
- Takes Bathsheba to be his wife:
  2 Samuel 11:26, 27
- Is rebuked by the prophet Nathan:
  2 Samuel 12:1-14
- Repents of his crime and confesses
  his guilt: Psalm 6; 32; 38; 39; 40;
  51
- Death of his infant son:
  2 Samuel 12:15-23
- Solomon is born:
  2 Samuel 12:24, 25

- David's flees from Jerusalem:
2 Samuel 15:13-37
- Absalom's defeat and death:
2 Samuel 18
- Laments the death of Absalom:
2 Samuel 18:33; 19:1-4
- Returns to Jerusalem:
2 Samuel 20:1-3
- Buries Saul's bones, and the bones of
his sons: 2 Samuel 21:12-14
- Defeats the Philistines: 2 Samuel
21:15-22; 1 Chronicles 20:4-8
- Counts the military strength of Israel
without divine authority, and is
reproved: 2 Samuel 24;
1 Chronicles 21; 27:24
- Solomon appointed to the throne:
1 Kings 1; 1 Chronicles 23:1
- Last words of: 2 Samuel 23:1-7
- Death of: 1 Kings 2:10;
1 Chronicles 29:28; Acts 2:29, 30

David's character

- His devotion to God: 1 Samuel
13:14; 2 Samuel 6:5, 14, 18; 7:18-
29; 8:11; 24:25; 1 Kings 3:14;
1 Chronicles 17:16-27; 29:10; 2
Chronicles 7:17; Zechariah 12:8;
Psalm 6; 7; 11; 13; 17; 22; 26; 27:7-
14; 28; 31; 35; 37
- Administers justice: 2 Samuel 8:15;
1 Chronicles 18:14
- Is discreet: 1 Samuel 18:14, 30
- Is humble: 1 Samuel 24:7; 26:11;
2 Samuel 16:11; 19:22, 23
- Is merciful: 2 Samuel 19:23
- David as musician: 1 Samuel 16:21-

23; 1 Chronicles 15:16; 23:5;
2 Chronicles 7:6; 29:26;
Nehemiah 12:36; Amos 6:5
- David as poet: 2 Samuel 22
- David as prophet: 2 Samuel 23:2-7;
1 Chronicles 28:19;
Matthew 22:41-46; Acts 2:25-38; 4:25
- David as a type of Christ: Psalm 2; 16;
18:43; 69:7-9
- Jesus called son of: Matthew 9:27;
12:23; 15:22; 20:30, 31; 21:9; 22:42;
Mark 10:47, 48; Luke 18:37, 39
- Prophecies concerning him and his
kingdom: Numbers 24:17, 19; 2
Samuel 7:11-16; 1 Chronicles 17:9-
14; 22; 2 Chronicles 6:5-17; 13:5;
21:7; Psalm 89:19-37; Isaiah 9:7;
16:5; 22:20-25; Jeremiah 23:5; 33:15-
26; Luke 1:32, 33
- A prophetic name for Christ:
Jeremiah 30:9; Ezekiel 34:23, 24;
37:24, 25; Hosea 3:5

Studying David with the psalms

It is not always possible to link up the
psalms David wrote with a specific
incident in his life. But where this is
possible one good way to study David's
life is to read the incident in David's life
and the relevant psalm with it.

For example the title to Psalm 51 reads,
"For the director of music. A psalm of
David. When the prophet Nathan came
to him after David had committed
adultery with Bathsheba." Some Bibles
provide helpful cross-references to these
titles. In this instance the cross-reference
is 2 Samuel 11:4; 12:1.

Peter

Also called Simon Bar-Jona and Cephas:
Matthew 16:16-19; Mark 3:16;
John 1:42.

Life of Peter

- A fisherman: Matthew 4:18;
  Luke 5:1-7; John 21:3
- Call of: Matthew 4:18-20;
  Mark 1:16-18; Luke 5:1-11
- His mother-in-law healed: Matthew
  8:14; Mark 1:29, 30; Luke 4:38
- An apostle: Matthew 10:2; 16:18,
  19; Mark 3:16; Luke 6:14; Acts 1:13
- An evangelist: Mark 1:36, 37
- Confesses Jesus to be the Messiah:
  Matthew 16:16-19; Mark 8:29;
  Luke 9:20; John 6:68, 69

His presumption

- In rebuking Jesus: Matthew 16:22,
  23; Mark 8:32, 33
- When the throng was pressing Jesus
  and the woman with the twelve year
  old blood disorder touched him:
  Luke 8:45
- In refusing to let Jesus wash Peter's
  feet: John 13:6-11

Present

- At the healing of Jairus' daughter:
  Mark 5:37; Luke 8:51
- At the transfiguration: Matthew
  17:1-4; Mark 9:2-6; Luke 9:28-33;
  2 Peter 1:16-18
- In the garden of Gethsemane:
  Matthew 26:36-46; Mark 14:33-42;
  Luke 22:40-46

Seeks the interpretation

- Of the parable of the steward:
  Luke 12:41
- Of the law of forgiveness:
  Matthew 18:21
- Of the law of defilement:
  Matthew 15:15
- Of the prophecy of Jesus concerning
  his second coming: Mark 13:3, 4
- Walks upon the water of Lake
  Galilee: Matthew 14:28-31
- Sent with John to prepare the
  Passover meal: Luke 22:8
- Calls attention to the withered fig
  tree: Mark 11:21
- His treachery foretold by Jesus, and
  his profession of being faithful:

Matthew 26:33-35; Mark 14:29-31; Luke 22:31-34; John 13:36-38
- Cuts off the ear of Malchus: Matthew 26:51; Mark 14:47; Luke 22:50
- Follows Jesus to the high priest's palace: Matthew 26:58; Mark 14:54; Luke 22:54; John 18:15
- His denial of Jesus, and his repentance: Matthew 26:69-75; Mark 14:66-72; Luke 22:55-62; John 18:17, 18, 25-27

After Jesus' death

- Visits Jesus' empty tomb: Luke 24:12; John 20:2-6
- Jesus sends message to, after the resurrection: Mark 16:7
- Jesus appears to: Luke 24:34; 1 Corinthians 15:4, 5
- Present at Lake Tiberias when Jesus appeared to his disciples; jumps into the water, and comes to shore when Jesus is recognized; is commissioned to feed the flock of Christ: John 21:1-23

As leader in the early church

- Lives in Jerusalem: Acts 1:13
- His statement in front of the disciples concerning the death of Judas, and his recommendation that the vacancy in the apostleship is filled: Acts 1:15-22
- Preaches on Pentecost day: Acts 2:14-40
- Heals the man at the gate of the temple: Acts 3
- Accused by the council; his defense: Acts 4:1-23
- Foretells the death of Ananias and Sapphira: Acts 5:1-11
- Imprisoned and scourged; his defense before the council: Acts 5:17-42
- Goes to Samaria: Acts 8:14
- Prays for the reception of the miraculous gifts of the Holy Spirit: Acts 8:15-18
- Rebukes Simon, the sorcerer, who desires to purchase this power: Acts 8:18-24
- Returns to Jerusalem: Acts 8:25
- Receives Paul: Galatians 1:18; 2:9
- Visits Lydda; heals Aeneas: Acts 9:32-34
- Visits Joppa; stays with Simon, the tanner; raises Dorcas from the dead: Acts 9:36-43
- Has a vision of a sheet containing ceremonially clean and unclean animals: Acts 10:9-16
- Receives the servant of the centurion; goes to Caesarea; preaches and immerses the centurion and his household: Acts 10
- Advocates the preaching of the gospel to the Gentiles in the hearing of the apostles and elders: Acts 11:1-18; 15:7-11
- Imprisoned and rescued by an angel: Acts 12:3-19
- Writes two letters: 1 Peter 1:1; 2 Peter 1:1

Paul

Early life of Paul

- Also called Saul: Acts 8:1; 9:1; 13:9
- From the tribe of Benjamin: Romans 11:1; Philippians 3:5
- Personal appearance of: 2 Corinthians 10:1, 10; 11:6
- Born in the city of Tarsus: Acts 9:11; 21:39; 22:3
- Educated at Jerusalem under Gamaliel: Acts 22:3; 26:4
- A zealous Pharisee: Acts 22:3; 23:6; 26:5; 2 Corinthians 11:22; Galatians 1:14; Philippians 3:5
- A Roman citizen: Acts 16:37; 22:25-28
- Persecutes the Christians; present at, and gives consent to, the stoning of Stephen: Acts 7:58; 8:1, 3; 9:1; 22:4
- Sent to Damascus with letters for the arrest of Christians: Acts 9:1, 2
- His vision and conversion: Acts 9:3-22; 22:4-19; 26:9-15; 1 Corinthians 9:1; 15:8; Galatians 1:13; 1 Timothy 1:12, 13
- Is baptized: Acts 9:18; 22:16
- Called to be an apostle: Acts 22:14-21; 26:16-18; Romans 1:1; 1 Corinthians 1:1; 9:1, 2; 15:9; Galatians 1:1, 15, 16; Ephesians 1:1; Colossians 1:1; 1 Timothy 1:1; 2:7; 2 Timothy 1:1, 11; Titus 1:1, 3
- Preaches in Damascus for the first time: Acts 9:20, 22
- Is persecuted by the Jews: Acts 9:23, 24
- Escapes by being let down from the wall in a basket; goes to Jerusalem: Acts 9:25, 26; Galatians 1:18, 19
- Received by the disciples in Jerusalem: Acts 9:26-29
- Goes to Caesarea: Acts 9:30; 18:22
- Sent to the Gentiles: Acts 13:2, 3, 47, 48; 22:17-21; Romans 11:13; 15:16; Galatians 1:15-24
- Has Barnabas as his companion: Acts 11:25, 26
- Teaches at Antioch (in Syria) for one year: Acts 11:26
- Brings the contributions of the Christians in Antioch to the Christians in Jerusalem: Acts 11:27-30
- Returns with the apostle John to Antioch (in Syria): Acts 12:25

First missionary tour

- Visits Seleucia: Acts 13:4
- Visits the island of Cyprus: Acts 13:4
- Preaches at Salamis: Acts 13:5
- Preaches at Paphos: Acts 13:6
- Sergius Paulus, governor of the country, is a convert of: Acts 13:7-12
- Contends with Elymas (Bar-Jesus) the sorcerer: Acts 13:6-12
- John (Mark), a companion of, departs for Jerusalem: Acts 13:13
- Visits Antioch (in Pisidia), and preaches in the synagogue: Acts 13:14-41
- His message received by the Gentiles: Acts 13:42, 49
- Persecuted and expelled: Acts 13:50, 51

- Visits Iconium, and preaches to the Jews and non-Jews; is persecuted; escapes to Lystra; goes to Derbe: Acts 14:1-6
- Heals a cripples: Acts 14:8-10
- The people attempt to worship him: Acts 14:11-18
- Is persecuted by Jews from Antioch and Iconium, and is stoned: Acts 14:19; 2 Corinthians 11:25; 2 Timothy 3:11
- Escapes to Derbe, where he preaches the gospel, and returns to Lystra, and to Iconium, and to Antioch, strengthens the disciples, exhorts them to continue in the faith, and helps to appoint elders: Acts 14:19-23
- Re-visits Pisidia, Pamphylia, Perga, Attalia and Antioch, in Syria, where he lived: Acts 14:24-28
- Contends with the Judaizers against their false teaching about the necessity of circumcision: Acts 15:1, 2
- Refers the question of circumcision to the apostles and elders at Jerusalem: Acts 15:2, 4
- He declares to the apostles at Jerusalem the miracles and wonders God had performed among the Gentiles thorugh them: Acts 15:12
- Returns to Antioch, accompanied by Barnabas, Judas and Silas, with letters to the Gentiles: Acts 15:22, 25
- Makes his second missionary tour: Acts 15:36

Second missionary tour

- Chooses Silas as his companion, and passes through Syria and Cilicia, strengthening the congregations: Acts 15:36-41
- Visits Lystra; circumcises Timothy: Acts 16:1-5
- Goes through Phrygia and Galatia; is forbidden by the Holy Spirit to preach in Asia; visits Mysia; attempts to go to Bithynia, but is restrained by the Spirit: Acts 16:6, 7
- Goes to Troas, where he has a vision of a man saying, "Come over into Macedonia, and help us"; immediately goes to Macedonia: Acts 16:8-10
- Visits Samothracia and Neapolis; comes to Philippi, in Macedonia; visits a place of prayer by the river; preaches the word; the merchant, Lydia, from Thyatira, is converted and baptized: Acts 16:11-15
- Drives out the evil spirit from the girl who practises fortune-telling: Acts 16:16-18
- Persecuted, beaten and thrown into prison with Silas; sings songs of praise in the prison; an earthquake shakes the prison; he preaches to the frightened jailer, who believes, and is baptized along with his household: Acts 16:19-34
- Is released by the civil authorities on the grounds that he is a Roman citizen: Acts 16:35-39; 2 Corinthians 6:5; 11:25; 1 Thessalonians 2:2

- Is welcomed at the household of Lydia: Acts 16:40
- Visits Amphipolis, Apollonia and Thessalonica; preaches in the synagogue: Acts 17:1-4
- Is persecuted: Acts 17:5-9; 2 Thessalonians 1:1-4
- Escapes to Berea by night; preaches in the synagogue; many Jews and Greeks believe: Acts 17:10-12
- Persecuted by the Jews who come from Thessalonica; is escorted by some of the brethren to Athens: Acts 17:13-15
- Debates on Mars' Hill (at the meeting of the Areopagus Council) with Greeks: Acts 17:16-34
- Visits Corinth; lives with Aquila and his wife, Priscilla (Prisca), who were tentmakers; joins in their trade: Acts 18:1-3
- Debates in the synagogue every Sabbath; is rejected by the Jews; turns to the Gentiles; makes his home with Justus; continues there for 18 months, teaching the word of God: Acts 18:4-11
- Persecuted by Jews, hauled up before Gallio, accused of breaking the law; accusation dismissed; takes his leave after many days, and sails to Syria, accompanied by Aquila and Priscilla: Acts 18:12-18
- Visits Ephesus, where he leaves Aquila and Priscilla; enters into a synagogue, where he debates with the Jews; starts his return trip to Jerusalem; visits Caesarea; crosses over the country of Galatia and Phrygia, strengthening the disciples: Acts 18:18-22

Third missionary tour

- Returns to Ephesus; lays his hands upon the disciples, who are baptized with the Holy Spirit; preaches in the synagogue; remains in Ephesus for two years; heals the sick people: Acts 19:12
- Rebukes the exorcists; drives out an evil spirit out from a man, and many believe, bringing their evil books of sorcery to be burned: Acts 19:13-20; 1 Corinthians 16:8, 9
- Sends Timothy and Erastus into Macedonia, but he himself remains in Asia: Acts 19:21, 22
- The spread of the gospel through his preaching interferes with the trade in idols; he is persecuted, and Ephesus is in uproar; the city clerk appeases the people; dismisses the accusation against Paul, and disperses the people: Acts 19:23-41; 2 Corinthians 1:8; 2 Timothy 4:14
- Goes to Macedonia after strengthening the Christians in that region; comes into Greece and lives for three months; returns through Macedonia, accompanied by Sopater, Aristarchus, Secundus, Gaius, Timothy, Tychicus and Trophimus: Acts 20:1-6
- Visits Troas; preaches until daybreak; restores to life the young

man (Eutychus) who fell from the window: Acts 20:6-12
- Visits Assos, Mitylene, Chios, Samos, Trogyllium and Miletus, hastening to Jerusalem, to be there by Pentecost day: Acts 20:13-16
- Sends for the elders of the congregation of Ephesus; relates to them how he had preached in Asia and his temptations and afflictions, urging repentance toward God: Acts 20:17-21
- Declares he was going bound in spirit to Jerusalem; warns them to be on the lookout for wolves who will attack the flock; kneels down, prays and leaves: Acts 20:22-38
- Visits Cos, Rhodes and Patara; boards a ship bound for Tyre: Acts 21:1-3
- Waits at Tyre for seven days; is brought by the disciples to the boundary of the city; kneels down and prays; boards the ship; comes to Ptolemais; greets the brethren and stays for one day: Acts 21:4-7
- Goes to Caesarea; visits the home of Philip the evangelist; is told by the prophet Agabus not to go to Jerusalem; nevertheless, he leaves for Jerusalem: Acts 21:8-15
- Is welcomed by the brethren; talks about the things that had been done among the Gentiles through his ministry: Acts 21:17-25

"When we arrived at Jerusalem, the brothers received us warmly… Paul greeted them" 21:17, 19.

Arrest, shipwreck and imprisonment

- Enters the temple courtyard, the people are stirred up against him by some Jews from Asia; an uproar is created; the commander of the Roman garrison intervenes and arrests him: Acts 21:26-33
- His defense: Acts 21:33-40; 22:1-21
- Is held in the fortress: Acts 22:24-30
- Is brought before the Sanhedrin; his defense: Acts 22:30; 23:1-5
- Is returned to the fortress: Acts 23:10
- Is encouraged by a vision from God, promising him that he will witness in Rome: Acts 23:11
- Jewish leaders plot to kill him: Acts 23:12-15
- This plan is thwarted by Paul's nephew: Acts 23:16-22
- Is escorted to Caesarea under heavy military guard: Acts 23:23-33
- Is confined in Herod's Judgment Hall in Caesarea: Acts 23:35
- His trial before Governor Felix: Acts 24
- Remains in custody for two years: Acts 24:27
- His trial before Governor Festus: Acts 25:1-12
- Appeals to be heard by Caesar: Acts 25:10-12
- His examination before Herod Agrippa II: Acts 25:13-27; 26
- Is taken to Rome in the custody of Julius, a centurion and a detachment of soldiers; boards a

ship, accompanied by other prisoners, and sails via the coasts of Asia; stops at Sidon, and at Myra: Acts 27:1-5
- Transferred to an Alexandrian ship; sails via way of Cnidus, Crete, Salamis and the Fair Havens: Acts 27:6-8
- Predicts misfortune of the ship; his counsel not heeded, and the voyage resumes: Acts 27:9-13
- The ship is caught in a storm; Paul encourages and comforts the officers and crew; the soldiers advise putting the prisoners to death; the centurion interferes and all on board, 276 people, survive: Acts 27:14-44
- The ship runs aground and all on board land on the island of Malta: Acts 27:14-44
- Treated well by the people of Malta: Acts 28:1, 2
- Is bitten by a viper and miraculously unharmed: Acts 28:3-6
- Heals the ruler's father and others: Acts 28:7-10
- Is delayed in Malta for three months; continues the voyage; delayed at Syracuse; sails via Rhegium and Puteoli: Acts 28:11-13
- Meets some brethren who accompany him to Rome from Appii Forum; arrives at Rome; is taken to the captain of the guard: Acts 28:14-16
- Summons the local Jewish leadership; preaches about the kingdom of heaven: Acts 28:17-29
- Lives under house arrest in his own rented house for two years, preaching and teaching: Acts 28:30, 31

Paul's character

- Supports himself: Acts 18:3; 20:33-35
  "He was a tentmaker as they were, he stayed and worked with them" 18:3.
- Sickness of, in Asia: 2 Corinthians 1:8-11
- His resolute determination to go to Jerusalem despite repeated warnings: Acts 20:22, 23; 21:4, 10-14
- Caught up to the third heaven: 2 Corinthians 12:1-4
- Has "a thorn in the flesh": 2 Corinthians 12:7-9; Galatians 4:13, 14
- His independent nature: 1 Thessalonians 2:9; 2 Thessalonians 3:8
- Persecutions of: 1 Thessalonians 2:2; Hebrews 10:34
- Persecutions endured: Acts 9:16, 23-25, 29; 16:19-25; 20:22-24; 21:13, 27-33; 22:22-24; 23:10, 12-15; Romans 8:35-37; 1 Corinthians 4:9, 11-13; 2 Corinthians 1:8-10; 4:8-12; 6:4, 5, 8-10; 11:23-27, 32, 33; 12:10; Galatians 5:11; 6:17; Philippians 1:30; 2:17, 18; Colossians 1:24; 1 Thessalonians 2:2, 14, 15; 3:4; 2 Timothy 1:12; 2:9, 10; 3:11, 12; 4:16, 17

7 TOPICAL BIBLE STUDIES

CONTENTS

Introduction

Jerusalem is the "holy city" for three great world religions: Christianity, Judaism and Islam. The significance of Jerusalem in both the Old and New Testaments is now highlighted. Because of the events with which it was associated it came to symbolize important spiritual truths. Jerusalem was linked in the Old Testament with God's protection of his followers, and with peace, and in the New Testament it was a symbol of the Church on earth, and the glorified Church in heaven.

The Bible does not set out to be an encyclopedia on music, or on birds, animals, reptiles and insects, or on flowers, shrubs and trees. However, there is a wealth of information on these topics in the Bible. The writers of the Bible draw out a surprisingly large number of spiritual truths from God's creatures and his creation. Jesus himself referred to birds of the air, sparrows, hens and vultures. And why did the Holy Spirit descend on Jesus at his baptism in the form of a dove? This chapter gives illuminating Bible studies on these topics.

Jerusalem

History of the city

The history of Jerusalem spans 15 centuries, from the time of Joshua to its destruction by Titus. It endured a succession of changes, revolutions, sieges, surrenders and famines. Each was followed by restoration and rebuilding. Its greatest glory was reached in King Solomon's reign when he built a magnificent temple, a sumptuous royal palace and enlarged and strengthened the walls of the city. Jerusalem was the most important city in Israel's history because it was preeminently God's city.

In about 1000 BC, Jerusalem became Israel's political and religious center. After Israel split into two kingdoms, Jerusalem remained the capital of the southern kingdom of Judah before it was destroyed by the Babylonians in 586 BC. After the Jews returned to Jerusalem from their exile in Babylonia the temple and the walls of Jerusalem were rebuilt.

Jerusalem was besieged and destroyed by the Romans in AD 70 when over 600,000 Jews were killed.

Names of Jerusalem

The names given to Jerusalem illustrate how central the city was to the Jews, to Jesus and to the early Christians.

Salem, Genesis 14:18, where Melchizedek was king; it was even in those days known as the royal city.

The Jebusite city, that is Jerusalem, Joshua 18:28. At the time of the conquest of Canaan, Jerusalem was attacked by both Judah and Benjamin, but the Jebusites regained control of it.

City of David, 2 Samuel 5:7; Isaiah 22:9. When David captured Jerusalem it was probably about 11 acres in size, with a population of about 3,500.

City of Judah, 2 Chronicles 25:28.

City of God, Psalm 46:4; 87:3. Psalm 48 depicts Jerusalem as a place of security which is impregnable from all points of attack, verses 2, 7, 10, 13.

Zion, Psalm 48:12.

Faithful city, which then acted like an unfaithful wife, Isaiah 1:21.

City of Righteousness, Isaiah 1:26.

City of our festivals, Isaiah 33:20. The three annual festivals of

described in these terms because of God's presence there.

Jerusalem in the time of Jesus

In AD 30 Jerusalem was dominated by Herod's temple which had been started in 19 BC and covered over 15% of the total area of Jerusalem. Besides being the center for Jewish worship in Jesus' day, it was the focus for Jesus' last week and the events which went to make up God's plan of salvation for humankind.

Going up to Jerusalem

Jesus made it quite clear that Jerusalem would be the setting for his death and resurrection: "We are going up to Jerusalem, and everything that is written by the prophets about the Son of Man will be fulfilled. He will be turned over to the Gentiles. They will mock him, insult him, spit on him, flog him and kill him. On the third day he will rise again." *Luke 18:31-33*

Jerusalem illustrates

The church, Galatians 4:25, 26; Hebrews 12:22, 23, when it refers to living Christians.

The glorified church, Hebrews 11:10, 16; Revelation 3:12; 21:2, 10.

God's protection of his followers, Psalm 125:2: "As the mountains surround Jerusalem, so the Lord surrounds his people both now and for evermore."

Peace, Psalm 122: 6, 7.

Passover, Weeks (Pentecost) and Tabernacles took place in Jerusalem.

City of the Lord, Isaiah 60:14. Other names for the future Jerusalem are found in Isaiah 1:26; 62:4; Ezekiel 48:35; Zechariah 8:3 and Hebrews 12:22.

City No Longer Deserted, Isaiah 62:12.

The Throne of the Lord, Jeremiah 3:17. The Lord was enthroned between the cherubim above the ark, 1 Samuel 4:4, but Jeremiah promises that one day Jerusalem will be God's throne.

City of truth, Zechariah 8:3.

Holy city, Nehemiah 11:1.

Holy hill, Daniel 9:16.

The perfection of beauty, Lamentations 2:15. Jerusalem is

Music in the Bible

Musical instruments

There is a wealth of teaching in the Bible about music and singing God's praises. Most of the music-making mentioned in the Bible is linked to worhiping God.

There are a wide variety of musical instruments found in the Bible:

Trumpet, Psalm 98:6
Cymbals, 2 Samuel 6:5
Harps, Genesis 4:21
Tambourine, Genesis 31:27
Horns, flute, zither, lyre, pipes,
  Daniel 3:5

Choirs

In David's day some choirs wore robes, 1 Chronicles 15:27, and some were accompanied by an orchestra, 1 Chronicles 9:33.

Singing God's praises

Perhaps the central theme about singing in the Bible is in connection with praising God.

1. The psalms

The psalms, Israel's hymn-book, are full of instructions about singing and encouragements to sing God's praises. "Come let us sing for joy to the Lord." *Psalm 95:1*

2. The prophets

Isaiah says, "And you will sing as on the night you celebrate a holy festival" Isaiah 30:29.

3. The New Testament

James says, in reply to his rhetorical question: "Is anyone happy? Let him sing songs of praise" James 5:13.

Paul talks about singing with his mind, 1 Corinthians 14:15, and tells the Ephesians: "Speak to one another with psalms, hymns and spiritual songs." And people who cannot sing in tune are not excluded, for everyone is told to, "Sing and make music in your heart to the Lord" Ephesians 5:19.

Music illustrates...
1. Joy and gladness

When the prophet Zephaniah wanted to say how much delight the Lord would take in his people he said, "He will rejoice over you with singing" Zephaniah 3:17.

2. Praise

David provided 4,000 people to praise the Lord with their musical instruments, 1 Chronicles 23:5.

3. A glimpse of heaven

John is shown pictures of heaven in the book of Revelation, and one of them depicts the 24 elders each having a harp and singing a new song to the Lamb (Jesus), Revelation 5:8, 9. "And they sang, a new song" 5:9.

Animals in the Bible and learning from them

God's care of the animals

The Bible reveals that God's care extends beyond humankind to the animal kingdom. This is detailed in Psalm 104.

> "He makes springs pour water into the ravines; it flows between the mountains.
> They give water to all beasts of the field; the wild donkeys quench their thirst." *Psalm 104:10, 11*

Sheep

Sheep are used to illustrate different things in the Bible and on occasions they symbolize diametrically opposite things.

1. God's people

God's people are referred to as "the sheep of your [God's] pasture" Psalm 74:1. In Psalm 23 the Lord is pictured as the psalmist's shepherd, caring for his sheep. The Lord being Israel's shepherd frequently occurs in the Old Testament: Psalm 28:9: 79:13; 80:1; 95:7; 100:3; Genesis 48:15; Isaiah 40:11; Jeremiah 17:16; 31:10; 50:19; Ezekiel 34:11-16.

2. Jesus' followers

Jesus says of himself that he is the shepherd of his people in his famous passage about him being the "Good Shepherd" John 10:11, 14. This theme is picked up in Hebrews 13:20; 1 Peter 5:4 and Revelation 7:17.

3. Evil people

The psalmist also depicts wicked people being like sheep. "Like sheep they are destined for the grave, and death will feed on them" Psalm 48:14.

4. The unregenerate

Jesus referred to Jews who did not believe in him as "the lost sheep of Israel" Matthew 10:6.

5. Restored sinners

In his parable of the one lost sheep, Luke 15:5, 7, Jesus speaks about "the lost sheep" who was found by the caring shepherd.

Wolf

Wolves are always used to stand for something that is evil.

Jesus sends out his 12 disciples like sheep among wolves, Matthew 10:16, and he describes those who attack his flock as being like wolves, John 10:12. Paul uses a similar metaphor when speaking of "savage wolves" who will not spare the flock, Acts 20:29.

Fox

Jesus once likened the cunning of King Herod to a fox, Luke 13:32.

Deer

One of the most inspiring and beautiful images about animals is drawn by the psalmist as he describes a person's longing for God.

"As the deer pants for streams of water, so my soul pants for you, O God." Psalm 42:1, 2.

"My soul thirsts for God"

Plants and trees in the Bible and learning from them

Trees and fruitfullness

The psalmist in Psalm 1:3 paints a similar picture to Jeremiah in depicting the happy stand of the righteous. Like a tree it withstands buffeting winds and provides shade and fruit for animals as well as humans.

"Blessed is the man who trusts in the Lord, whose confidence is in him.
He will be like a tree planted by the water that sends out its roots by the stream.
It does not fear when heat comes; its leaves are always green.
It has no worries in the year of drought and never fails to bear fruit." *Jeremiah 17:8*

The vine

In the Old Testament the vine often stands for Israel. "Israel was a spreading vine," Hosea 10:1. So when Jesus told his parable about a landowner who planted a vineyard and who, after the tenants had behaved like murderers, gave the vineyard to other tenants, it is hardly surprising that Matthew adds by way of conclusion the reaction this had on some who were listening. "When the chief priests and the Pharisees heard Jesus' parables, they knew he was talking about them." *Matthew 21:45*

The cedars of Lebanon

These trees had spreading branches that could grow up to 100 feet long. The psalmist states that the righteous can grow like cedars, Psalm 92:12.

Olive trees

Olive trees were grown for their oil which was used in cooking and as fuel for lamps, for grooming the hair and skin and for religious rites. It was a most useful tree, for in addition to its fruit, which did not appear until it was 15 years old, its wood was used for building, as Solomon did in building the temple. The psalmist declared: "But I am like an olive tree flourishing in the house of God; I trust in God's unfailing love for ever and ever" Psalm 52:8.

The lilies of the field

Jesus said, "And why do you worry about clothes? See how the lilies of the field grow" Matthew 6:28, teaching how wrong it is to be anxious since we are cared for by our heavenly Father.

In his *The Lilies of the Field and the Birds of the Air*, Søren Kierkegaard wrote in 1849, "What is to be the man...oh, that we might learn this...from the lilies and the birds...So in accordance with the directions of the Gospel let us consider seriously the lilies and the birds as teachers and imitate them."

The tree of life

In Genesis 3:22 we read about a tree planted in Eden whose fruit would enable Adam and Eve to live forever. But after their sin and the Fall they were driven out from Eden and the route back to the tree of life was guarded by a cherubim and his flaming sword, Genesis 3:24.

The book of Revelation also mentions this tree of life which stands for everlasting life for the godly. The faithful of the church at Ephesus are promised the right to eat from the tree of life, Revelation 2:7. The last chapter of the New Testament expands on this by giving the following details about this tree of life: "On each side of the river stood the tree of life, bearing twelve crops of fruit, yielding its fruit every month. And the leaves of the tree are for the healing of the nations" Revelation 22:2. In Revelation 22:14 it is those who have washed their robes [and so are made righteous in God's sight] that may have the right to the tree of life.

Birds in the Bible and learning from them

Many varieties

There are more than 20 varieties of birds mentioned in the Bible.

- Black vulture
- Cormorant
- Dove
- Great owl
- Hawk
- Hoopoe
- Little owl
- Ostrich
- Quail
- Red kite
- Sparrow
- Swallow
- White owl
- Black kite
- Desert owl
- Eagle
- Gull
- Heron
- Horned owl
- Osprey
- Pigeon
- Raven
- Screech owl
- Stork
- Vulture

See Genesis 15:9; Exodus 16:13; Leviticus 11:13-19; Deuteronomy 14:11; Job 39:13; Psalm 84:3.

Spiritual lessons

The authors of the Bible point to particular spiritual lessons which can be drawn from some of the birds. Two of them, the eagle and the dove, are often singled out in this way.

Security

The psalmist pictures birds making their nests where they will be safe, in the branches of the very tall cedars of Lebanon, Psalm 104:17.

Proverbs 27:8 likens a man wandering away from the security of his home to a bird that strays from its nest. "Like a bird that strays from its nest, is a man who strays from his home."

Learning from the dove
The Holy Spirit

At Jesus' baptism the Holy Spirit came down on him like a dove, Matthew 3:16.

Israel

The psalmist uses the picture of a dove that has its wings sheathed with silver and its feathers coated with shining gold, Psalm 68:13, to stand for Israel and how God will bring them success in battle and receive the plunder of war.

The prophet Hosea describes Ephraim like a dove which is senseless and easily deceived, Hosea 7:11.

Mourners

The prophet Isaiah likens mourners to the moans of doves, Isaiah 38:14; 59:11. "We moan mournfully like doves."

Peace and life

As the flood receded a dove was sent out of the ark and returned with an olive branch in its beak, Genesis 8:11. This symbol is used to depict peace today.

Learning from the eagle
God's care

God tells Moses that his care for his people is like a female eagle who carries its young on its wings, Exodus 19:4.

The temporary nature of riches

Proverbs 23:5 advises us to only have a quick glance at riches as they quickly disappear, as if they sprout wings like eagles and soar away into the sky.

Spiritual renewal

Eagles were renowned for their vigor, so the psalmist can promise that God can renew people so that they become like a young, strong eagle, Psalm 103:5. Eagles were also well known for their speed. The prophet Jeremiah likens galloping horses to the speed of eagles in flight: "his horses are swifter than eagles" Jeremiah 4:13.

Isaiah reminds his hearers that God does not tire and that those who trust him will be inwardly renewed.

"Even youths grow tired and weary,
    and young men stumble and fall;

but those who hope in the Lord will
    renew their strength.
They will soar on wings like eagles;
    they will run and not grow weary,
    they will walk and not be faint."
Isaiah 40:30, 31

Jesus and the birds
1. The dove and innocence
Jesus told his 12 disciples that they were to be as innocent as doves, Matthew 10:16.

2. The birds and God's care
Jesus told his hearers that the God who is concerned about each sparrow and who feeds all the birds of the air also keeps watch over all humankind, Matthew 6:25-27.

Commenting on this passage from the Sermon on the Mount, Martin Luther wrote in 1521, "You see, he is making the birds our school-masters and teachers. In other words, we have as many teachers and preachers as there are little birds in the air."

3. The wings of a hen
Jesus uses the image of a hen gathering her chicks under her wings as a symbol of God's powerful protection, Matthew 23:37.

4. Vultures around a carcass
Jesus said that his second coming would be as clear as the sight of vultures gathering around a carcass for a meal, Matthew 24:28.

Is the Bible infallible?

Before we can answer this question we need to understand what the Bible is. Many things have been said against the Bible. Can it be historically reliable? What about all its contradictions? Aren't reason and tradition more important than the Bible? How can a 2,000-year-old book be our guide in our scientific age? Who says your particular interpretation of the Bible is the right one? Bible scholars can't even agree among themselves about the Bible! How can a book written by uneducated people like fishermen and shepherds be inspired by God?

In the face of such searching questions how can Christians insist that the Bible is totally trustworthy?

What the Bible is *not*

The Bible is not *primarily* a history book. Yes, it does contain a great deal of history, especially about the Jews, but it is highly selective in the material it uses.

The Bible is not *primarily* a geography book. Yes, it does tell much about the land of Judah, and scores of archaeological digs support its accuracy, but the Bible does not set out to be a sort of *National Geographical Magazine* of Bible lands.

The Bible is not *primarily* a scientific book. Yes, it does contain profound ideas about such things as the creation of the world which eminent scientists down the ages, such as Isaac Newton, Robert Boyle, James Simpson and Michael Faraday, accepted, but the Bible does not answer the question *How was the world made?* so much as the question *Who made the world?* and *Why?*

The Bible is not *primarily* a work of great literature. Yes, it does contain many highly acclaimed writings, such as the book of Job, which Tennyson called "the greatest poem of ancient and modern times," but the Bible was not just meant to be read as wonderful literature.

What is the theme of the Bible?

The Bible may consist of 66 books, but it has one, unifying theme: salvation.

The focus of the Scriptures

Amazing as it may seem, people manage to read the Bible and miss its main theme. The focus of the whole Bible is on God the Father and Jesus Christ. Jesus once told the Jews, "the scriptures ...testify about me" (John 5:39).

Christ in the law
The first five books of the Bible, the Pentateuch, were known as the books of the law in Jesus' day. Moses made the following prediction which was exactly fulfilled by Jesus: "The Lord your God will raise up for you a prophet like me from among your own brothers. You must listen to him...The Lord said to me...'I will put my words in his mouth, and he will tell them everything I command him.'" *Deuteronomy 18:15, 18*

The first words in Mark's Gospel about Jesus' public ministry is the Greek word for "fulfilled" *peplerotai,* "The time has come,...the kingdom of God is near" (Mark 1:15).

Christ in the prophets
Jesus fulfills the prophets' desire for peace and justice. "For to us a child is born, to us a son is given, and the government will be on his shoulders. And he will be called Wonderful Counsellor, Mighty God, Everlasting Father, Prince of Peace." *Isaiah 9:6*

Christ in the writings
The third division of the Old Testament scriptures in Jesus' day was known as "the Writings," (the Psalms and the wisdom books). At Jesus' baptism and transfiguration the words used of him

came from Psalm 2:7, "you are my Son." (See Matthew 3:17; Luke 9:35.)

As Martin Luther said, "The whole of Scripture deals with Christ throughout."

Christ in the New Testament
Every New Testament book centers on Jesus Christ. At the end of his Gospel John says that he wrote so that his readers might have faith in Jesus. "Jesus did many other miraculous signs in the presence of his disciples, which are not recorded in this book. But these are written that you may believe that Jesus is the Christ, the Son of God, and that by believing you may have life in him." *John 20:30, 31*

The Bible is a book about God
If you want to find out about God, "Read the Bible," says the Christian. Here are some of the important characteristics of God taught in the Bible.

1. God is holy. Revelation 4:8
2. God is the Creator. Genesis 1:1
3. God is Spirit. John 4:24
4. God is invisible. John 1:18
5. God is personal. John 17:1-3
6. God is all-powerful. Revelation 19:6
7. God is merciful. Lamentations 3:22, 23
8. God is all-knowing. 1 John 3:20
9. God is omnipresent. Psalm 139:7-12
10. God is wise. Acts 15:18
11. God is infinite. 1 Kings 8:27
12. God is eternal. Isaiah 57:15
13. God is patient. Exodus 34:6, 7

14. God is true. Revelation 15:3

15. God is loving. 1 John 4:8, 16

Christianity is a revealed religion. Christians believe that the record of God's revelation to humankind is in the Bible.

The Bible is the revealed Word of God

In the Old Testament alone phrases like, "God spoke to Moses," "the word of the Lord came to Jonah," and "God said," come over two thousand times. If we want to know about God and eternal matters we find the way revealed in the Bible.

Does this mean we can know every-thing there is to know about God?

No. The Bible does not tell us about *everything*, but just about those things which God has decided to tell us. "The secret things belong to the Lord our God, but the things revealed belong to us and to our children for ever, that we may follow all the words of this law." *Deuteronomy 29:29*

Does this mean that all our problems are solved?

No. There are some questions, like the problem of the innocent suffering of babies, that we may never have complete answers to.

Does this mean that we can understand everything in the Bible?

No. When Billy Graham was interviewed on TV by David Frost he was asked, "Do you still have difficulties with the Bible?"

The elderly Billy Graham answered, "I still have dozens of things I don't understand in the Bible. But I know that they'll all be solved in heaven."

Does this mean that the Bible answers our modern ethical problems?

No, in the sense that there is no verse to look up in the Bible which says that cloning a sheep is right or wrong.

But, yes, in the sense that the Bible provides all the principles by which we need to live. For example, one basic Bible principle is that the weak, poor and vulnerable in our society should be especially taken care of. This principle can then be applied to such questions as abortion and euthanasia.

What about reason?

Christians have been created rational beings. Peter says, "Always be prepared to give an answer to everyone who asks you to give the *reason* for the hope that you have," 1 Peter 3:15. But reason is not to be pre-eminent. For who would have said that one man dying on a cross two thousand years ago could bring God's forgiveness to us today?

What about tradition?

There are scores of positive traditions which Christians keep. Here is the aging apostle Paul giving his "last will and testament" to Timothy. "What you have heard from me, keep as the pattern of sound teaching, with faith and love in

Christ Jesus. Guard the good deposit that was entrusted to you – guard it with the help of the Holy Spirit who lives in you," 2 Timothy 1:13, 14. However, ritual or man-made traditions need to be distinguished from "sound teaching" which is to be safeguarded.

What happens if the Bible and tradition clash?

Jesus pointed out what we must do if a human tradition clashes with God's word. He warned the Pharisees not to "nullify the word of God for the sake of your tradition" (Matthew 15:6).

Who wrote the Bible?

The Bible is human, yet divine. Its 66 books were written over a period of some 1,400 to 1,600 years by as many as 40 different people.

The authors of the Bible were divinely inspired. "For prophecy never had its origin in the will of man, but men spoke from God as they were carried along by the Holy Spirit." *2 Peter 1:21*

So, is the Bible infallible then?

God is infallible. Perhaps a more revealing question is: Is our understanding of the Bible infallible?

The love *of Scripture*

Rewarding Bible studies are found from studying one particular important word in the Bible. If the verses you read are written out the wonder of the Bible's teaching is often increased. A straightforward Bible study is to look up some of the key verses on the theme of love. You can then compile, in the words of the Bible, the Bible's teaching on this topic.

For God so loved the world that He gave His only begotten Son, that whoever believes in Him should not perish but have everlasting life. For God did not send His Son into the world to condemn the world, but that the world through Him might be saved. He who believes in him is not condemned. *John 3:16-18, NKJV*

He who loves his brother abides in the light, and there is no cause for stumbling in him. *1 John 2:10, NKJV*

Know therefore that the LORD your God is God; he is the faithful God, keeping his covenant of love to a thousand generations of those who love him and keep his commands. *Deuteronomy 7:9, NIV*

Confess your faults one to another, and pray one for another, that ye may be healed. The effectual fervent prayer of a righteous man availeth much. *James 5:16, KJV*

Be devoted to each other like a loving family. Excel in showing respect for each other. *Romans 12:10, GWT*

A new commandment I give to you, that you love one another; as I have loved you, that you also love one another. By this all will know that you are My disciples, if you have love for one another. *John 13:34-35, NKJV*

The LORD passed before him, and proclaimed, "The LORD, the LORD, a God merciful and gracious, slow to anger, and abounding in steadfast love and faithfulness, keeping steadfast love for the thousandth generation, forgiving iniquity and transgression and sin…" *Exodus 34:6, 7, NRSV*

And let us consider how we may spur one another on toward love and good deeds. *Hebrews 10:24, NIV*

Can a mother forget the baby at her breast and have no compassion on the child she has borne? Though she may forget, I will not forget you! See, I have engraved you on the palms of my hands. *Isaiah 49:15, 16, NIV*

For I am persuaded that neither death nor life, nor angels nor principalities nor powers, nor things present nor things to come, nor height nor depth, nor any other created thing, shall be able to separate us from the love of God which is in Christ Jesus our Lord. *Romans 8:38, 39, NKJV*

For this reason I bow my knees to the Father of our Lord Jesus Christ, from whom the whole family in heaven and earth is named, that He would grant you, according to the riches of His glory, to be strength-ened with might through His Spirit in the inner man, that Christ may dwell in your hearts through faith; that you, being rooted and grounded in love, may be able to comprehend with all the saints what is the width and length and depth and height— to know the love of Christ which passes knowledge; that you may be filled with all the fullness of God. *Ephesians 3:14-19, NKJV*

He who has My commandments and keeps them, it is he who loves Me. And he who loves Me will be loved by My Father, and I will love him and manifest Myself to him. *John 14:21, NKJV*

But the steadfast love of the LORD is from everlasting to everlasting upon those who fear him, and his righteousness to children's children. *Psalm 103:17, RSV*

Dear friends, we must love each other because love comes from God. Everyone who loves has been born from God and knows God. The person who doesn't love doesn't know God, because God is love. God has shown us his love by sending his only Son into the world so that we could have life through him. This is love: not that we have loved God, but that he loved us and sent his Son to be the payment for our sins. Dear friends, if this is the way God loved us, we must also love each other. *1 John 4:7-11, GWT*

The Synoptic problem

What is the Synoptic problem?

Synoptic

The word *synoptic* is made up of two parts. *Syn,* meaning "together with." *Opitic,* meaning "seeing." So the word *synoptic* means "seeing together."

In marked contrast to John's Gospel, the first three Gospels present a "common view" of the facts about Jesus implied in the Greek word *synopsis*, "a blended view."

Three "synoptic" Gospels

The Gospels of Matthew, Mark and Luke are sometimes called the "synoptic" Gospels.

A careful reading of the four Gospels quickly reveals that Matthew, Mark and Luke are similar to each other and have a very different feel to them from John's Gospel.

Matthew, Mark and Luke have:

- a similar viewpoint
- similar material
- a similar order of the events and sayings of Jesus
- similar characteristics.

Look at the statistics

1. Matthew's Gospel contains over 90% of the verses found in Mark's Gospel.
2. Luke's Gospel contains over 50% of the verses found in Mark's Gospel.
3. Unique material to Matthew, 7%, Mark 59%, Luke 7%, John 92%.

4. Only 31 verses of Mark's Gospel have no parallel in Matthew's or Luke's Gospel.
5. Matthew and Luke each have about 250 verses not paralleled in Mark.
6. About 300 verses in Matthew's Gospel and about 250 verses in Luke's Gospel have no parallel in any of the other Gospels.

The Synoptic problem

Where did the authors of the synoptic Gospels obtain their material from?

- Were the authors dependent on each other as they wrote their Gospels?
- Did the authors go to a common source for their material?

These kinds of questions concerning the original make-up of each of the first three Gospels are now called the Synoptic problem.

Theories galore

The idea about Q is not the only theory alive today.

Q STANDS FOR *QUELLE*

The verses in Matthew's Gospel and in Luke's Gospel which are common to each other, but do not appear in Mark's Gospel are often called "Q" material.

Quelle (Q) is the German word for "source."

The theory is that Q, along with Mark's Gospel, was used by Matthew and Luke as they compiled their Gospels.

Other suggestions about the origin of the Gospels include:

1. The priority of Matthew
This view says that Mark and Luke drew on Matthew's Gospel as they wrote. This theory assumes that Matthew's Gospel was written before Mark's and Luke's.

2. The existence of oral tradition
This view states that all the Gospel writers used a well-known, oral source about the life of Jesus, that had been passed on by word of mouth.

3. The lost Gospel
This view suggests that the Gospel writers had access to another Gospel, which no longer exists.

4. Written fragments
This idea believes that short records about Jesus' actions and words were made during his life, and that the Gospel writers had access to them and used them.

5. A combination of various theories
Some scholars think that the Gospel writers made use of oral tradition, written fragments and each other's writings, as well as eyewitnesses whom they spoke to.

Divine inspiration is not affected
No matter how the synoptic Gospels may have been originally written by Matthew, Mark and Luke, Christians have always believed:

- that the Holy Spirit guided the thinking and writing of the Gospels writers;
- that every part of all the Gospels are divinely inspired;
- that the Gospels are part of Scripture and that "all Scripture is God breathed." *2 Timothy 3.16*

Similar aims
Hypotheses galore
One of the tantalizing problems about scholarly attempts to unravel exactly how each Gospel came to be written is that nobody knows for certain how it happened. There are many variations on the Synoptic problem and it is always important to bear in mind that each is only a hypothesis. Often today's latest hypothesis looks very tired and dated after only a few years.

Luke's stated aim
"…it seemed good to me to write an orderly account for you, most excellent Theophilus, so that you may know the certainty of the things you have been taught." *Luke 1:3, 4*

John's stated aim
"Jesus did many other miraculous signs… These [Jesus' miraculous signs] are written that you may believe that Jesus is the Christ, the Son of God, and that by believing you may have live in his name." *John 20:30, 31*

8 MEMORIZING THE BIBLE AND BIBLE STUDY ON THE INTERNET

Introduction

In New Testament times the synagogue school was an established part of Jewish life. From the age of six Jesus would have gone to the synagogue school in Nazareth where he would have joined the semi-circle of boys who sat on the floor facing the rabbi. Much of the teaching was done by repetition and memorizing. Jewish schools required each student to master several key passages of Scripture, passages such as Deuteronomy 6:4, 5; 11:13-21 and Numbers 15:37-41. When Jesus was tempted in the desert he rebutted the devil's temptations with three quotations from the book of Deuteronomy: Deuteronomy 8:3; 6:16 and 6:13 "Fear the Lord you God." Clearly Jesus knew these off by heart.

This section explains how one can profitably start memorizing Bible verses. It also shows how the practice can become a habit for life.

For anyone who is interested in using the Internet for Bible study, a few key addresses from the worldwide web are given. From these you will be able to access scores of different Bibles, Bible dictionaries, Bible concordances and other Bible study aids.

Memorizing the Bible

Getting started

If you have tried to remember Bible verses and gave up, don't worry. Just start again.

If you have never tried to memorize Scripture before, don't be put off. It could be a great plus for you in your Christian life.

The reason most Christians don't memorize anything in an organized way from the Bible is that they just don't start. So get started now.

Be motivated

People memorize great chunks of Shakespeare. Christians have the best possible motives for memorizing Scripture:

- It can help us to bring glory to God
- It can help other people
- It can help us.

Here are three reasons for memorizing Scripture:

Be someone who can correctly handle the Bible

"Do your best to present yourself to God as one approved, a workman who does not need to be ashamed and who correctly handles the word of truth." *2 Timothy 2:15*

Be someone who studies the Bible

"For Ezra had devoted himself to the study and observance of the Law of the LORD, and to teaching its decrees and laws in Israel." *Ezra 7:10*

Be someone who delights in the Bible

"Blessed is the man who does not walk in the counsel of the wicked or stand in the way of sinners or sit in the seat of mockers. But his delight is in the law of the LORD, and on his law he meditates day and night. He is like a tree planted by streams of water, which yields its fruit in season and whose leaf does not wither. Whatever he does prospers." *Psalm 1:1-3*

Be warned

A great deal of what is written about memorizing Scripture focuses on the mechanical side of remembering verses. This is fine. But remember that this is only a means to an end. Some people become spiritually proud that they have remembered 100 verses or 1,000 verses. The point about memorizing Scripture is a spiritual one. Never lose sight of that. We should grow as Christians when we memorize Scripture because we become more obedient to God and live more holy lives.

Some tips about memorizing Scripture

Go slow
It is much better to start slowly and be accurate in your memory work than to half remember lots of Bible verses. Quality is much more important than quantity.

Select a Bible
From the scores of Bible translations you need to select one version for your memory work. It's best to memorize from just one Bible version. Use a Bible that you really like and find reasonably easy to understand. It's better to use an accurate Bible translation like the *New International Version* than to go for a bright new paraphrase.

Establish a routine
Set aside a time when you devote yourself to this memory work. If you think that you will do this when you have time you may never start, or if you do start you may quickly give up. If you can do this first thing in the morning, just for ten minutes, you'll be amazed by the progress you will make.

Learning your first verse
Say you decide to learn John chapter 3 verse 16.

Read the whole verse over a few times. Look at where it comes in John chapter 3, so that you can know a little bit about its context. As you do this you will see that it comes at the conclusion of Jesus' conversation with one of the leading rabbis, Nicodemus.

Break up the verse into little chunks that you find easy to remember.

> For God so loved
> the world
> that he gave
> his one and only Son,
> that whoever believes in him
> shall not perish
> but have everlasting life.

Then memorize the Bible reference: "John 3 16" stands for John chapter 3 verse 16.

- Now read the verse again. Now, if you are able to, read the verse out aloud.
- Now read just the first phrase: "For God so loved…"
- Now read the second phrase: "the world…"
- Now read the first two phrases.
- Now read the third phrase and then the first three phrases, until you are reading the whole verse.
- Keep doing this until you have learned the verse and its reference.

100%
Remember, you are not interested in anything less than 100% accuracy.

Which verses shall I memorize?

Variety is the spice of life

You may have some favorite Bible verses, so why not start with them?

As you read the Bible and come across other verses you would like to memorize make a note of them on a piece of paper that you keep in your Bible.

If you just don't know where to start, try some "3:16" verses, that is some Bible verses that are all from chapter 3 and verse 16.

Here are some excellent ones:

- Proverbs 3:16, about wisdom
- Malachi 3:16
- Acts 3:16
- 1 Corinthians 3:16
- Colossians 3:16
- 1 Timothy 3:16
- 2 Timothy 3:16

Writing out the verses

A handy way to keep track of the verses you are learning is to write them on blank business cards.

At the top of the card write out a heading which summarizes the verse for you. In the case of John 3:16 it might be, "God's love." Then underline this heading.

Underneath the heading write out the verse you are learning. Make sure that it is word perfect.

On the bottom right hand of the card write out the Bible reference: John 3:16

On the bottom left hand of the card write out a heading that a group of verses can be known by. In this instance it could be "3:16 verses." If you learn the above eight verses, then number them in order. If you learn John 3:16 first, then on the card write "3:16. 1" If you learn Proverbs 3:16 as your second verse in this series of verses on the bottom left hand of that card write "3:16. 2" and so on.

"Long life is in her right hand;
in her left hand are riches and honor"
Proverbs 3:16.

"Don't youknow that you yourselves are God's temple and that God's spirit lives in you? *1 Corinthians 3:16*

Other series of verses to remember

On the following pages, pages 186-190, you will find one verse which has been selected from each book of the Bible. You may not want to write all the verses out on cards yet. So you can just use these pages as they are to learn from.

Reviewing verses

On Saturday, don't memorize any new verses, just review the verses you have learned.

It's been said that you have not really memorized any verse until you have reviewed it 100 times!

Memorizing longer Bible passages

Go for passages that you may already be acquainted with, or for passages which are especially wonderful.

Psalm 23 verses 1-6 is not too difficult to memorize.

Romans 8: verses 1-39 is much more challenging to learn.

More tips

1. Try one syllable at a time

If you want to memorize Romans 8:1, try saying it to yourself, and out aloud, as follows:

"There - fore, - there - is - now - no - con - demn - ation - for - those - who - are - in - Christ - Jesus."

2. Use the gaps in the day

It has been estimated that we spend seven years waiting in queues! Make use of times like this to review some Bible verses. Also make use of this time to meditate on the last Bible verse you committed to memory.

3. Other ideas for topics to memorize

Why not collect together promises from the Bible and remember them, one by one.

Review, review, review

When you have remembered your first verse, move on and remember your second verse. But before you go on to your third verse, review your second verse. This means repeat it to yourself to make sure that you can remember it. And don't forget that it must be word perfect. And don't forget to say its reference at the end. Then recite your first two verses. Now you are ready for your third verse.

Make a habit of not adding to your memorized verses until you have successfully reviewed the verses you know.

On Sunday have a complete rest from reviewing and Bible memory work.

Golden verses

PART ONE: THE OLD TESTAMENT		
Memorizing one verse from each Bible book in the *King James Version*.		
Book	*Topic*	*Scripture verse and reference*
Genesis	Creation	"In the beginning God created the heaven and the earth" 1:1.
Exodus	Redeemed	"I will redeem you with a stretched out arm, and with great judgments" 6:6.
Leviticus	Holiness	"Sanctify yourselves therefore, and be ye holy: for I am the Lord your God" 20:7.
Numbers	God's mercy	"The Lord is longsuffering, and of great mercy, forgiving iniquity and transgression" 14:18.
Deuteronomy	A godly walk	"And now, Israel, what doth the Lord thy God require of thee, but to fear the Lord thy God, to walk in all his ways, and to love him" 10:12.
Joshua	Meditation	"This book of the law shall not depart out of thy mouth; but thou shalt meditate therein day and night" 1:8.
Judges	Turning from God	"In those days there was no king in Israel: every man did that which was right in his own eyes" 21:25.
Ruth	Loyalty	"And Ruth said, Intreat me not to leave thee, or to return from following after thee: for wither thou goest, I will go; and where thou lodgest, I will lodge: thy people shall be my people, and thy God my God" 1:16.
1 Samuel	Obedience	"Behold, to obey is better than sacrifice, and to hearken than the fat of rams" 15:22.
2 Samuel	God's ways	"For I have kept the ways of the Lord, and have not wickedly departed from my God" 22:22.
1 Kings	Prayer for wisdom	"Give therefore thy servant an understanding heart to judge thy people, that I may discern between good and bad" 3:9.
2 Kings	Fear not	"And he answered, Fear not: for they that be with us are more than they that be with them" 6:16.
1 Chronicles	God's majesty	"Thine, O Lord, is the greatness, and the power, and the glory, and the victory, and the majesty: for all that is in the heaven and in the earth is thine; thine is the kingdom, O Lord, and thou art exalted as head above all" 29:11.

2 Chronicles	God's sight	"For the eyes of the Lord run to and fro throughout the whole earth to shew himself strong in the behalf of them whose heart is perfect toward him" 16:9.
Ezra	A prepared heart	"For Ezra had prepared his heart to seek the law of the Lord, and to do it, and to teach in Israel statutes and judgments" 7:10.
Nehemiah	Prayer and action	"Nevertheless we made our prayer unto God, and set a watch against them day and night" 4:9.
Esther	God's timing	"…who knoweth whether thou art come to the kingdom for such a time as this?" 4:14.
Job	Faith during suffering	"For I know that my redeemer liveth" 19:25.
Psalms	A clean heart	"Create in me a clean heart, O God; and renew a right spirit within me" 51:1.
Proverbs	Reverence	"The fear of the Lord is the beginning of knowledge: but fools despise wisdom and knowledge" 1:7.
Ecclesiastes	Our duty	"Fear God, and keep his commandments: for this is the whole duty of man" 12:13.
Song of Solomon	Love	"Many waters cannot quench love, neither can the floods drown it" 8:7.
Isaiah	Wounded for me	"But he was wounded for our transgressions, he was bruised for our iniquities." 53:5.
Jeremiah	Inner law	"I will put my law in their inward parts, and write it in their hearts" 31:33.
Lamentations	Hope	"The Lord is my portion, saith my soul; therefore will I hope in him" 3:24.
Ezekiel	Inner power	"And I will put my spirit within you, and cause you to walk in my statutes" 36:27.
Daniel	Inner revelation	"He revealeth the deep and secret things" 2:22.
Hosea	Like the dew	"I will be as the dew unto Israel: he shall grow as the lily, and cast forth his roots as Lebanon" 14:5.
Joel	God's Spirit	"And it shall come to pass afterward, that I will pour out my spirit on all flesh: and your sons and your daughters shall prophesy, your old men shall dream dreams, your young men shall see visions" 2:28.

PART ONE: THE OLD TESTAMENT *cont.*		
Book	*Topic*	*Scripture verse and reference*
Amos	Restoration	"And I will plant them upon their land, and they shall no more be pulled up out of their land which I have given them" 9:15.
Obadiah	Humbled	"Though thou exalt thyself as an eagle, and though thou set thy nest among the stars, thence will I bring thee down, saith the Lord" 4.
Jonah	God's kindness	"I knew that thou art a gracious God, and merciful, slow to anger, and of great kindness" 4:2.
Micah	A humble walk	"What doth the Lord require of thee, but to do justly, and to love mercy, and to walk humbly with thy God?" 6:8.
Nahum	God's goodness	"The Lord is good, a strong hold in the day of trouble; and he knoweth them that trust in him" 1:7.
Habakkuk	Faith	"The just shall live by faith" 2:4.
Zephaniah	Seek God	"Seek ye the Lord, all ye meek of the earth" 2:3.
Haggai	Covenant love	"According to the word that I covenanted with you when ye came out of Egypt, so my spirit remaineth among you: fear ye not" 2:5.
Zechariah	A regal ride	"Rejoice greatly, O daughter of Zion; shout, O daughter of Jerusalem: behold, thy King cometh unto thee: he is just, and having salvation; lowly, and riding upon an ass, and upon a foal of an ass" 9:9.
Malachi	Healing	"Unto you that fear my name shall the Sun of Righteousness arise with healing in his wings; and ye shall go forth, and grow up as calves of the stall" 4:2.

PART TWO: THE NEW TESTAMENT		
Memorizing one verse from each Bible book in the *King James Version*.		
Book	*Topic*	*Scripture verse and reference*
Matthew	Mission	"Go ye therefore, and teach all nations, and, lo, I am with you alway, even unto the end of the world. Amen" 28:19, 20.
Mark	A ransom	"For even the Son of Man came not to be ministered unto, but to minister, and to give his life a ransom for many" 10:45.
Luke	The lost	"For the Son of man is come to seek and to save that which was lost" 19:10.
John	The world	"For God so loved the world, that he gave his only begotten Son, that whosoever believeth in him should not perish, but have everlasting life" 3:16.
Acts	Spiritual growth	"So mightily grew the word of God and prevailed" 19:20.
Romans	Peace with God	"Therefore being justified by faith, we have peace with God through our Lord Jesus Christ" 5:1.
1 Corinthians	Charity	"And now abideth faith, hope, charity, these three; but the greatest of these is charity" 13:13.
2 Corinthians	Light	"For God, who commanded the light to shine out of darkness, hath shined in our hearts, to give the light of the knowledge of the glory of God in the face of Jesus Christ" 4:6.
Galatians	Crucified	"I am crucified with Christ: nevertheless I live; yet not I, but Christ liveth in me: and the life which I now live in the flesh I live by the faith of the Son of God, who loved me, and give himself for me" 2:20.
Ephesians	Grace	"For by grace you have been saved through faith; and that not of yourselves: it is the gift of God" 2:8.
Philippians	God's peace	"And the peace of God, which passeth all understanding, shall keep your hearts and minds through Christ Jesus" 4:7.
Colossians	Work as for God	"And whatsoever ye do, do it heartily, as to the Lord, and not unto men" 3:23.
1 Thessalonians	God's faithfulness	"Faithful is he that calleth you, who also will do it" 5:24.

2 Thessalonians	Stand fast	"Therefore, brethren, stand fast, and hold the traditions which ye have been taught, whether by word, or our epistle" 2:15.
1 Timothy	The godly road	"Follow after righteousness, godliness, faith, love, patience, meekness" 6:11.
2 Timothy	Power and love	"For God hath not given us the spirit of fear; but of power, and of love, and of a sound mind" 1:7.
Titus	God's grace	"For the grace of God that bringeth salvation hath appeared to all men" 2:11.
Philemon	A brother	"Receive him for ever; not now as a servant, but above a servant, a brother beloved" 15, 16.
Hebrews	Surrounded	"Wherefore seeing we also are compassed about with so great a cloud of witnesses, let us lay aside every weight, and the sin which doth so easily beset us, and let us run with patience the race that is set before us" 12:1.
James	Endurance	"Blessed is the man that endureth temptation" 1:12.
1 Peter	The cross	"Who his own self bare our sins in his own body on the tree, that we, being dead to sins, should live unto righteousness: by whose stripes ye are healed" 2:24.
2 Peter	Temptation	"The Lord knoweth how to deliver the godly out of temptations" 2:9.
1 John	God's love	"This then is the message which we have heard of him, and declare unto you, that God is light, and in him is no darkness at all" 1:5.
2 John	This is love	"And this is love, that we walk after his commandments" 6.
3 John	Good and evil	"Beloved, follow not that which is evil, but that which is good" 11.
Jude	Kept from falling	"Now unto him that is able to keep you from falling, and to present you faultless before the presence of his glory with exceeding joy..." 24.
Revelation	I will come in	"Behold, I stand at the door, and knock: if any man hear my voice, and open the door, I will come in to him, and will sup with him, and he with me" 3:20.

The Bible and Bible study on the Internet

Top sites

From the following Internet address all the other addresses mentioned on these two pages can be accessed.

> **Web address:**
> *http://www.biblestudytools.net/*
> **Title:** Goshen Bible Study Tools
> **Features include:** Bibles; search

This site says of itself: "The Goshen Bible Study Tools/Online Study Library is designed to be a resource that facilitates in-depth study and exploration of God's Word and that fosters a desire to learn more about the Bible and how to apply it to our lives."

Searching Bible versions

From the opening page found on *http://www.biblestudytools.net/* you have immediate access to the following Bible versions:

- *Today's English Version*
- *New King James Version*
- *King James*, with Strong's numbers
- *American Standard Version*
- *New American Standard Version*
- *Revised Standard Version*
- *Douay-Rheims*
- Bible in Basic English
- Darby Translation
- Young's Literal Translation.

Any word in the Bible

You can search for any word or phrase in any of these Bible versions.

Or you can look up any Bible verse in any of these versions.

Searching for a topic

From the opening page found on *http://www.biblestudytools.net/* you have immediate access to search for a topic of your choice.

The following comprehensive Bible dictionaries and Bible concordances are now at your fingertips:

- Eastern's Bible Dictionary
- Hitchcock's Bible Name Dictionary
- Nave's Topical Bible
- Strong's Exhaustive Concordance
- Torrey's New Topical Textbook.

These Bible study tools are cross-indexed.

These books have huge lists, and sort a great many Scripture references into thousands of different topics and categories.

The interlinear Bible

> **Web address:** *http://www.biblestudy tools.net/InterlinearBible/*
> **Title:** Interlinear Bible
> **Features include:** Bibles; search

At the above Internet address you have the choice of viewing:

- The Hebrew–English Old Testament
- The Greek–English New Testament

This site explains how you can view the Greek and Hebrew text on screen. If you search for "Genesis 1:1" or for "John 1:1" the English version of that verse comes up on your screen, with the Hebrew or Greek underneath it. Any verse from the Bible can be viewed in this way.

Lexicons

Web address: *http://www.biblestudy tools.net/lexicons/*
Title: Bible lexicons
Features include: Bibles; search

The above address gives you access to either a Hebrew lexicon or to a Greek lexicon.

It gives you the facility to browse through the lexicon, or to choose any Hebrew or Greek word.

The Greek lexicon is based on *Thayer's and Smith's Bible Dictionary,* as well as others. It is also keyed to the *Theological Dictionary of the New Testament.*

The Hebrew lexicon is *Brown, Driver, Briggs, Gesenius* lexicon, and is also keyed to the *Theological Dictionary of the Old Testament.*

Bible commentaries

Web address: *http://www.biblestudy tools.net/commentaries/*
Title: Bible commentaries
Features include: Bibles; search

The Bible commentaries on line from this address include:

- Geneva Study Bible
- Jamieson, Fausset, Brown Bible Commentary
- Treasury of Scripture Knowledge
- John Wesley's Explanatory Notes
- Darby's Synopsis of the New Testament.

You can access commentary on any verse in any book of the Bible from these commentaries and compare two or more with each other.